DESMOND RYAN

MICHAEL COLLINS

ANVIL BOOKS

First published as *The Invisible Army*
by Arthur Baker Ltd., London, in 1932
Published by Anvil Books in 1968
Sixth reprinting 1985

ISBN 0 900068 00 0

Printed in Ireland by Mount Salus Press

*With the exception of the 1916 leaders, Michael
Collins and a few others, obvious to all who know the
period 1916–1924, the characters in this book are
fictitious, and no reflection is made or implied on any
living person – Desmond Ryan 1932*

CHAPTER I

ON Easter Monday morning, Nineteen Sixteen, small groups of Irish Volunteers gathered into a small drill hall on the Dublin quays opposite the Four Courts. From ten o'clock onwards a stream of grey-green uniformed men, of men in Sunday best, bent under the weight of rifles and harnessed in shoulder-straps, haversacks and water-bottles, of men in labouring garb armed with shot-guns and Martini rifles, of young lads in the kilts of the Fianna Eireann, passed through the narrow doorway in twos and threes.

Towards noon the door opened and Michael Collins swept out at the head of a small party, a rifle beneath his arm, his Cork accent vibrating. He and his men vanished into the network of lanes behind the hall. Tall and wiry, his jaw aggressively a-tilt, grey-blue eyes burning, Michael Collins vanished, the words floating back behind him:

> *We died for England from Waterloo,*
> *To Egypt and Dargai;*
> *And still there's enough for a corps or a crew.*
> *Kelly and Burke and Shea,*

Within a man's voice was drowned in a burst of cheering from the fifty-two Volunteers out of the company roll of three hundred who had answered the hurried mobilisation of the morning. For there had been a dramatic end to their long wait. As noon struck the Commandant in charge had strode forward and called the men to attention in a firm voice. He watched the ranks before him in silence for a few moments, his black eyes two rigid rays in the pallor of his thin face, a slight spare figure in grey-green, a light playing on the metal badge of his military cap, his fingers strumming on the Mauser revolver which dangled by his side.

In a level voice, which rose by degrees to a shout, he spoke, and all the rumours and presentiments which had haunted the city over the week-end, all the whispered conjectures of the waiting groups in that hall, became a blinding and numbing certainty, a dream of the poets translated into the Commandant's almost prosaic announcement:

"Men, I want you to listen to me for a few minutes, and no applause must follow my statement. TODAY, AT TWELVE NOON,

3

AN IRISH REPUBLIC WILL BE DECLARED. I only wish to add that communications with our other positions are precarious, and that in less than an hour we may be in action."

Away in the distance came a rattle of rifle-fire which seemed to fade into a circle of reports around the city. A far-off sound of cheering and heavier firing. A wild outcry filled the room and sank to whispers. Long had these men talked of revolution, and now it stood before them. Here and there a man shivered beneath the shock, a worried and haggard expression breaking over his face, while his comrades rallied him, but most of the men were in good spirits as the Commandant's ringing orders dispersed them into small parties, while the rattle of arms from the O'Connell Street area and beyond Dublin Castle grew sharper and louder. As the hall emptied, the Commandant came across to where Arthur Macken the electrician, Dick Blake the docker, and David Harding the reporter, were arguing with their fiery little friend Bernard Milroy the barber.

"I don't know you three men," he said quickly. "What company do you belong to?"

Bernard Milroy looked up and spoke:

"They belong to another battalion, friends of mine. They got no word from their own officers, and most of their company refused to come out after all the conflicting orders that's floating round. So I gave them the word to drop in here, for I guessed and they guessed there was something in the wind after the calling off of the All-Ireland manoeuvres yesterday."

The Commandant handed a dispatch to Arthur Macken and said:

"Well, you'll find your battalion in the G.P.O. Take this there with your friends, and Milroy can go with you. If he's more useful, he can stay. Resist any attempt to stop you. We may be cut off any time now. Good luck."

As the four men stepped out on the quays they saw that barricades were being hastily thrown across the streets—taxi-cabs, wagons, floats. The Volunteers were seizing houses at street corners, and all the glass in the windows fell tinkling on to the pavements before the vigorous blows of rifle-butts, while through all the din were heard the dull blows of picks and hammers boring and smashing through walls. Voices rang persistently: "Fill every vessel with water . . . a wall more bored is another life saved . . . keep under cover . . . no shooting without orders." Above on the roofs snipers and bombers scanned the quays. Slowly over the Four Courts rose and fluttered a flag: the Green, White and Orange of the Republic.

4

The four men went down the quays in silence. That bleak area now seemed to them alien to the Dublin they had known. A volley swept the cobbles at their feet as they approached O'Connell Bridge, and they turned into a side lane towards the Post Office. They halted in a doorway and looked at each other.

"So the fight is on," said David Harding, "and a mighty poor turn-out our crowd has made. Did any of you see the Tiger Doyle?"

"I went round to see him this morning," said Arthur Macken, smiling wryly, a cynical look in his grey eyes. "He knew all about the route-march order for today, but mumbled something about divisions among the leaders and stayed where he was."

"The curse of Jasus on him!" cried Dick Blake. "Always a fierce member taking the bloody Castle with his big scowling mouth. God send that the bloody military catch him and knock the lard criss-crossways in him!"

"Enough of that language, please," said Bernard primly. "Have we a chance, Arthur?" He shifted his enormous rifle, a trophy of the Howth gun-running, from one shoulder to the other, a mad gleam in his eyes.

"Yes," said Macken, "of funerals and glory. Come on now, boys."

One o'clock struck as they hurried into O'Connell Street. Volunteers were dashing across the thoroughfare towards the Post Office. A girl was led down a side-turning crying bitterly and deaf to all the appeals of a well-dressed young man beside her. A working man cheered wildly as the Volunteers dashed past and waved his cap: "Good men, give it to the bastards!" A party of Lancers appeared from behind the Parnell Monument and dashed down the street at full gallop. From the upper windows of the Post Office and adjoining houses a fusillade rang. And a second and a third. The working man ran for cover, spun round, and lay still on the pavement, a red pool oozing from under him. The Lancers returned the fire and wheeled to retreat. Suddenly Milroy left the cover of the doorways and ran madly up the street towards the plunging horses.

"Come on, lads!" he yelled. "Charge them!"

His bayonet jutted out above his gun, as large as he; there was a strained look in his blue eyes, and his sparse hair fluttered over his whitened face, and his cap tumbled in the dust behind. Before Macken's warning shout could reach him the little barber was sprawling riddled on the roadway. Again and again the volleys roared and rolled. Bullets spattered at the feet of Arthur Macken, and thirty other Volunteers crouched back in the sheltering doorways. Two hundred yards ahead, Republican tricolours were flapping above the graceful front of the General Post Office. The air was alive with the swift and hissing bullets. Two dead horses lay near a deserted tramcar at Nelson's Pillar. Beyond, Bernard Milroy and six others were stretched stone-dead. In the distance beat the hoofs of the Lancers' horses in retreat, some of the riders clinging to their chargers, groaning and a wild stare in their eyes. Along the quayside towards Dublin Castle and the Four Courts sounded further deadly bursts of gunfire. Macken headed his companions in a dash from cover and led them into Prince's Street to the great side gate of the Post Office.

Tense faces peered through windows behind sand-bags and planks.

"Who are you?" came the peremptory question from behind the barricades of sacks, tables and stout boarding in the lower windows. Macken questioned the party of Volunteers, many limp and bleeding, behind him and shouted:

"Havensfield Company, Fourth Battalion."

But the great side gate could not be opened, for in the turmoil the key had been mislaid. Again the bursts of gunfire from behind the Parnell Monument and an echo along the distant quays, while a bleak and vivid light brooded over all.

"Mind yourselves, the troops are returning!" yelled someone. . . .

"Line up!" cried another.

"Break the windows, you bloody fools!" roars Macken, and his rifle-butt dives into a shower of splintered wood and glass. A dozen rifle-butts circle madly above excited faces and the high windows crash and the wave of Volunteers goes through. A deafening noise and a groan and a man collapses on the pavement. Shot in the stomach with his own gun, he lies still.

Into a wild confusion of carrier-bicycles, vans, motor-cars, milk-churns, baskets and dustbins in the central yard surge the Volunteers. Macken, Harding and Dick Blake halt and look at the groups dashing to barricade hitherto undefended windows with sacks, books, boards, anything stout and bulky. Glass crashes and locks are blown in. Here and there rough coverings have been thrown over dead Volunteers. Outside continuous fusillading shakes the street, to be followed by an ominous lull in which crowds creep slowly back from the side lanes to gaze up at the groups of Volunteers on guard on the roof beneath the tricolours waving.

As the minutes pass, the interior grows more and more

orderly. A postal official in shirt-sleeves struggles into his coat and dashes for the entrance gate as it swings open to admit a cheering company of Volunteers.

"Let me out, for God's sake!" pleads the official, his face ashen.

"Oh, stop and join us, man!" shout the guards on duty at the makeshift barricade which covers the main gate.

"No, I must go home. I have a wife and family."

"Well, good luck!" cry the guards as he vanishes with terror in his eyes. "You would be safer in here, my lad!"

A florid and dazed Dublin Metropolitan policeman sits on a barrel, his face buried in his hands. Volunteers chaff him, and he sits up and asks for a drink, as he has five children and one wife.

"From us you'll get nothing but kindness," reply his captors, smiling broadly. "Angus Fitzsimmons the poet is in charge of the beer, and, begob, they say the supercilious bowsie has it emptied all down the sink already, and as for the hard stuff, he only hands it out to them with the death-rattle sounding in their throats."

"Hurrah, boys, hurrah!" shouts a young Volunteer officer, waving a greeting to friends as he runs towards the main hall. "There's a load of bombs at the door."

Reinforcements come and go. The garrison makes a formidable show. Some are glitteringly accoutred in trim grey-green, service rifle and automatic pistol, neatly rolled puttees, martial sabre, soldierly cap or dashing turned-up hat. Others—the majority—are merely in everyday garb, crossed and intercrossed with shoulder-straps, water-bottle, armed in many cases with shot-guns or miniature rifles. Around their left arms, as a distinctive badge, they wear bright yellow bands.

During a lull the body of Bernard Milroy was carried in. Macken and his two companions followed it into the hospital. In a sorting-room on the second floor, Cumann na mBan nurses had set up a dressing station. Outside the rattle of rifles and machine guns rang over the city's roofs. Death had come into his own, and the room gradually filled with the maimed and dying. Amid the piles of lint, bandages, splints and all the paraphernalia of healing heaped in neat rows and layers on tables and packed in countless pigeon-holes, at the feet of the keen-eyed officers and women lay the wounded. Here was stretched a powerful Volunteer with thoughtful face, semi-conscious, flat on his back, gasping for breath, his leaden eyes rarely moving. There another, pale and asleep, the blood

7

splashed over his bandaged head, and arm in splints. Yonder, again, a young boy, smiling with forced cheerfulness and muttering to himself.

The enthusiastic young lieutenant who had cried: "Hurrah, boys, hurrah!" so wildly fifteen minutes before is led in, blood streaming over his face and hands, the sequel to a careless handling of a bomb in the load at the door.

"Hush, hush!" comes in a tense whisper from a small side-room. "Two men are dying within."

Macken shook his head and looked down sadly on the jagged wounds in the jaw and forehead of Bernard Milroy. Dick Blake shrugged his shoulders and looked away. Harding sighed, and a stream of memories flashed and leaped around the rigid little form: talk in the little barber's shop, parades, fiery arguments in the little mill among the Dublin hills, a white yacht sailing into Howth Harbour and Milroy and himself in a crowd of Volunteers helping to land the thousand enormous 1871 German rifles, and Dublin Castle on Cork Hill abruptly awake to what was afoot . . . Scottish Borderers drawn up at Dollymount cross-roads . . . over the fields with the guns . . . winking tram conductors refusing fares . . . Borderers firing on stone-throwing crowds as they march back to the city . . . . "There'll be war now," says Bernard when the last of the twelve rifles have been stowed safe in his cellar and they chat in his tiny kitchen. . . .

Harding looked again at the dead body, and a shudder broke his thoughts. Then a sharp voice sounded in his ear:

"So you're here, lads! Half our company is on the roof. Go up, Arthur, and take charge. Dick Blake can go, too. He's a good sniper."

Sean Condron, their Company commander, lean figure alert and eyes alive beneath his bushy brows, stood beside them. He glanced down at Bernard and asked when they had entered the Post Office. He sent Harding across to the front windows, where the defenders stand waiting for that general assault which will never come. Pikes, daggers, trench knives and revolvers lay in readiness for a hand-to-hand struggle whenever the attackers might arrive and break through. Beside the guards at loop-holes were placed bowls of shot-gun ammunition as a reserve supply. Rumours of Ireland ablaze were as common as rosary beads around the necks of the defenders. Cork and Limerick and Kerry, the eager story ran, were rising in revolt; the Curragh line was held on both sides; submarines had sunk a hundred transports in the Irish Sea; and fifty thousand men were marching from the provinces to support the Dublin fighters.

"A great day for the poor!" cry the Volunteers when a ragged and wild-eyed army breaks out from the slums and looting begins. The plate-glass windows of a neighbouring sweet shop are shivered, and a mass of bright-coloured confectionery tosses among the crazy crowds. In vain Volunteer pickets appeal to the looters, a shoe store is rushed, the women of the slums hurling themselves at the heavy plate glass in a frenzy, laughing madly while the thick fragments scatter deep gashes. The Volunteer pickets remonstrate no more. Hard-eyed young men with revolvers and wooden batons charge the looters and deal sturdy blows. Men armed with fixed bayonets follow. Sean MacDermott limps across the street and calls with passion on the looters to disperse and not disgrace the first days of the Republic. A looter tears madly past, flinging a valise away in terror, the smack of a baton synchronising with the thud of the valise on the cobbles. The Volunteers fire three volleys over the looters' heads, and the street empties.

A working man spoke to Harding, who was watching the scene.

"Things are desperate, are they not? Liberty Hall anti-militarists and dreamy poets all in the one boat. Did you ever read my poems against war in Jim Larkin's *Worker*? You didn't, perhaps. I was all for the dove of peace, yet here I am with this bloody shot-gun!"

The remark appealed to Harding's own mood. He laughed and glanced at the crowds creeping back into the street, at a wisp of smoke curling up from a shop opposite, at the rows of armed guards in the houses across the street. A man on his left broke in:

"Now, Tom Hughes, cheer up! Sure, we all read your poems. And bloody fine poems they were. But the greatest men in the world don't know whether they're on their heads or their heels since the bloody war started. I was in the South African War myself. This is a mad bloody business. We should have took to the hills like the Boers, and not shut ourselves up here with all our leaders and three bloody flags over our heads to show where we were. Too damn honest altogether. There's always something, however. The Boers had old Cronje doing the softie. Would not pursue his flying enemy because of some text in his old Bible. I suppose he was a poet, too."

In the meantime, Macken had taken over his party on the roof. He ordered the position to be strengthened with boards and sandbags. He told his men not to fire without orders, and to avoid smoking when darkness fell. He had food served out, and watched the human ebbs and flows below. Once he shouted sharply:

"DON'T FIRE!"

A British soldier, astonished at the scene, had halted and looked up at the men on the roof. Women gathered round him and persuaded him to retrace his steps. Again Macken's sharp order. A British second lieutenant strolls unconcernedly down O'Connell Street, and looks up at the three flags of the Republic, high and proud in the air, topmost a green flag with "Irish Republic" emblazoned in yellow. A group of Volunteers surround the lieutenant. He puts his hands up and disappears into the building below. Macken inspects his men, warns them to be sparing of ammunition and not to load up without his leave. He chats with several recruits who have come in on the spur of the moment, or who have been only a few weeks in the Volunteers. He greets a Volunteer officer who comes up to tell them that no attack is expected that night. Bright green uniform; piercing eyes; pointed moustaches . . . where has he met the man? . . . "The O'Rahilly," says Sean Condron at his elbow, "against this; but 'in' all the same."

"British troops are swarming up from the Curragh," The O'Rahilly tells them both in a low tone. "The country has not risen. How could it when the arms landing failed? Only half the Dublin Brigade has come out owing to the muddle of orders, counter-orders and orders. Tomorrow the British will hold us in an iron grip. We are to hold out as long as the buildings last."

Darkness fell, but Macken could not sleep. The quiet roofs of the city spread out before him, the arc lamps droning along the noble thoroughfare. He lay on the cold slates and covered himself with his coat. From the Four Courts direction reverberated resounding and continuous volleys, a strange and almost cheering contrast to the darkened and subdued atmosphere which hung over the roof. The men paraded the parapet, screening cigarettes from observation or drinking tea from their billy-cans. Dawn rose at last above the sea of chimney-stacks, spires, towers and roofs.

Macken watches the hands of a clock below. The hands move in a swift circle which reduce hours to minutes and minutes to seconds and time to illusion. A few tired Volunteers drop off into an uneasy sleep, waxen and grime-stained. A warning is shouted and the whole garrison on the roof springs to arms and levels rifles across the sides and parapet. . . . A lull. . . . Another alarm. . . . The guards sink back again. . . . Clear day comes. A wild figure in blue fur-trimmed motor-coat with its face and hands blackened tramples down the sloping slates to shout the morning's mad tidings. It is Dick Blake. He starts as a bullet whistles past his black hat. He brandishes a revolver and raps out a whirling oath. The roof is reorganised. Rain falls and the stacks of tin-canister bombs are protected by sacking. In readiness along the ledge ammunition is placed, The O'Rahilly comes up with frequent inquiries as to reported advances of troops. A flame shoots up from a handsome store on the other side of the street, glows and roars skywards. A great clanging of fire bells and engines, brass helmets and ladders underneath, but the Fire Brigade retires as the flames spread beyond control and creep round house after house in the block.

A call rings over the roof:

SNIPERS NEEDED. SNIPER VOLUNTEERS FORWARD!

Macken, at a nod from Sean Condron, wraps himself in oil-skins and creeps higher above the slates, rifle in hand. He is glad to be relieved of his placid command in this timeless world where perpetual calls to arms break into snatched dreams and the circle of dark and dawn, the air now quivering with machine-guns tapping—tap-tap-tapping down O'Connell Street, bullets cutting grooves in the great porch under the parapet, men sinking with swift moans as the British snipers get the range of the roof. Macken lives again with a heated barrel in his hand, a distant impersonal target in that sea of sinister windows and roofs, the pattering bullets, the almost unconscious feeling that with this hot and ringing rifle he gambled with a lifetime's memory and blotted out another with each spinning and falling quarry. . . . A bullet grazes his hat. . . . He aims at a dark form outlined on the roof away in the Rotunda direction. . . . It spins groundwards, a rifle escaping from its grasp as it somersaults. . . . Bullets strike the chimney above him. . . . A scream below and a body rolls down the slates. . . . Hour after hour. . . .

He looked down and saw The O'Rahilly waving to him. He climbed back and received an order to go downstairs and rest. Sean Condron came up when he answered impatiently, and asked:

"Don't you realise, Arthur, that this is Wednesday evening?"

Macken went down iron ladders and winding stairways. Far above came a terrific series of explosions, the eternal tap-tap-tapping, screams and a grinding of slates.

"Roof swept by machine-guns!" said a passing Volunteer laconically. Looking back, Macken noticed Volunteers with Red Cross armlets going through the skylight.

11

Harding was on guard in the yard. They compared notes. As they watched in a darkened archway, there was one glaring circle of fire around them. Harding had the same story as his own minus the thrills of the sniper: the bullets which missed him at the windows, the eternal rumours, the flight of time and sleep from his world, the passing of fear since that morning's orchestra of artillery had shattered Liberty Hall near the Custom House and shaken the Post Office foundations. Redder and redder blazed one fiery block opposite.

Michael Collins, with dark rings under his eyes, his uniform torn and dusty, limped towards them. They all peered through the gate at some maddened horses which had broken loose from adjacent stables, at a cat which blinked with mad eyes at the flames, at a crazed and drunken man who staggered across the street and howled:

"Yous are Irishmen and if yous were bet tomorrow yous would be Irishmen still!" Brighter grew the spreading and hideous blaze, which murmured and throbbed, outlining every brick and stone.

Michael Collins shook his head and shrugged his shoulders and spoke half to himself:

"Perhaps we're done, boys. Fierce scrapping in the outlying districts. We hold Jacob's factory, Boland's Mill, the South Dublin Union, the College of Surgeons, and in short a ring of positions round the city, but the attack on the Castle failed. Not half the Dublin men came out."

His dark hair waved plume-like above his pale face and the strain in his grey-blue eyes. He went on:

"We left the Hall to look up some of the lads with orders to report back here. We gathered a half-dozen or so and got caught on the way back. The troops are pouring up from the Curragh and in from Kingstown. We took refuge in a house on the way in and saw a barricade in the street below. There was sniping from the windows. We heard our lads had held up the troops for hours. But when we arrived there was a great wave of khaki sweeping down the street. The firing from the windows died down, for the ammunition had given out. The fighting had maddened the troops, an inch advance for every hour, and madder and madder with every casualty. We had one rifle and two revolvers among the seven of us. We built a barricade on the stairs and prepared for the end. . . . They were stark mad when they broke through and captured the street barricade. . . . Young Doyle, you know, the Tiger's brother, was captured at the barricade after hurling a bomb, and they

12

shot him dead beside the cart-planks barricade. They shot rings round them, screaming at the top of their voices. They searched the houses and passed ours and went away. And then I saw a strange thing: in the windows across the way the Tiger Doyle himself looking down into the street, with a face as white as a fish's belly, on his dead brother below. The louser had funked it."

The story was interrupted by the arrival of Dick Blake. His left hand was bandaged. His face was stained with dirt and dark red splashes starred with rough medical dressings and marked with pain and sleeplessness.

"Hello, Mick, are you alive and kicking? Christ, there's hell to pay above since you came down, Arthur. The whole bloody kip is commanded by snipers and the roof has been swept by shrapnel. Two lads, too raw to take cover, have been shot through the head crossing the slates. The chimneys and the glass contraption on the top are the worse for the wear and tear. I got a crack myself as well as poor old Edward Malone. Still, we mustn't complain. But some of our own are hard to put up with! Do you know that fellow, Angus Fitzsimmons, the alleged poet who's in charge of the food? Do you know anything strange or wonderful about that old tub of guts with an accent you could hang your hat on? Eh? You don't? Well, then, for Jasus sake go up and have one good long laugh before the Devil his father gets him. Up I goes—wounded and all as you see me—and says I, 'Gimme me a bottle of stout for the love of Jasus,' says I, 'and something to eat,' says I. 'Drink watah,' says he, blinking at me like a bloody eagle down his long nose. 'Eat that crust!' says he, pointing at the heel of a loaf that'd blunt a crocodile's teeth. 'If you never had a decent bite in your life before, is that any reason why I should supply you with a four-course dinner before you die for Ireland? Mend your manners and don't parade your scars.' Jasus!"

Sean Condron joined the group and interrupted:

"Still at it, Dick?"

The four men wandered into the main hall. An officer with sleep-lorn eyes numbered off men for a sortie, and long lines of Volunteers stood to attention, two rows deep.

"Here's Pearse," whispered Macken, and a Volunteer Commandant, his eyes burning with enthusiasm, came forward, his deep voice ringing through the vast room. Harding's mind wandered back to the November night when he first heard Patrick Pearse speak to the crowds in the Rotunda Rink at the launching of the Irish Volunteers, and in that speech had sounded the stark directness some historian of Imperial Rome might have

13

put in the mouths of Ancient Britons flaunting a last defiance at Caesar's eagles. . . . A crash of gunfire, a rumble of falling houses, a rattle of rifles overhead. . . . Pearse's voice grew louder: Dublin would be for ever an heroic city like Paris of old. . . . The main positions were intact . . . other risings had taken place throughout the country . . . . They had defied England's might for three days . . . they would win through, though perhaps for many of them it would be in death. . . .

Harding looked at the wall beside him. The Republican Proclamation in deep black type hung there, and its glowing phrases reflected the speaker's passion and faith:

"IN THE NAME OF GOD AND OF THE DEAD GENERATIONS, FROM WHOM SHE RECEIVES HER AUGUST TRADITION OF NATIONHOOD, IRELAND, THROUGH US, SUMMONS HER CHILDREN TO HER FLAG AND STRIKES FOR HER FREEDOM." Half-glimpses of the men who had signed this last defiance came back to Harding even as Pearse's voice soared and sank and soared. . . . Sean MacDermott in the street awhile back, a sick man, limping out to reprove the looters. . . . Connolly smiling at his insurgent tricolours: "Isn't it grand?" waving later towards the booming guns: "they're beaten or they would never have shelled us." . . . Joseph Plunkett, as the bombardment heightened, walking down the lines of guards at the front windows with quaint bird-like stare: "Not since Moscow has a capital been burned."

The speech ended. Whispers attracted Harding's attention, and he looked round. A woman had halted beside Sean Condron. Harding nodded to her. It was Winifred Considine, sister of the poet, Dermott Considine, who was one of the Volunteer leaders. Considine lived out among the South Dublin hills in a ramshackle mansion where rumour said the Volunteers had made bombs and sheltered from the raiding parties in the days before the Rising. Two dark eyes were a burning contrast to the whiteness of her face, black hair gathered across her pensive forehead. The whispers startled Harding.

"No, not a word from Dermott since he left for Kerry . . . the landing failed. . . . We must get those documents . . . they would hang a hundred men. . . . There's still a chance. . . ."

Sean Condron drew a pencil and paper from his breast pocket and sketched a plan. . . . Winifred Considine moved away towards the main gate. . . . A general call to arms rings out, and the garrison goads itself to activity to repel the long-threatened general assault, while the roar of the heavy artillery grows as familiar as the hissing bullets and the staccato machine-gun bursts. Telephone communication breaks down with the

14

posts across the street, and as the fire grips those posts, one by one, men descend and race over the deadly spaces to the Post Office in twos and threes. Sometimes a racing figure halts, spins and drops half-way. BOOM, BOOM, BOOM. The walls and floors tremble, the dazed guards wait, wait, wait, their eyelids heavy. . . . Another evening darkens, and the street becomes one murmuring, leaping, orange blaze which laps the cool stars in the serene sky above.

Behind lurid barricades, three rows deep, the defenders kneel; the fiery circle lights up the outer walls and inner defences. Away through the flames sounds a chorus of doomed defiance:

> Tonight we man the Bearna Baoghail
> In Erin's cause, come woe or weal,
> Mid rifles' roar or cannons' peal
> We'll chant a Soldier's Song. . . .

From all quarters of the fire and darkness, the song rose and spread—defiantly sweeping all cares and fears before it. . . .

Once again Harding, on guard at the lower windows, saw the dawn. There was a lull till noon. Reports sped round that it was arbitration. The men gathered in the great yard and argued. A wild cry rang through the front room, a foreboding of evil, defeat and the end: the fire had at last gripped the Post Office.

Macken stood beside Harding with a grim look in his eyes:

"Go round and warn the officers in charge on this floor to hold their men in readiness to retire and then rejoin me on the roof. It's been hit by a petrol shell and blazing like mad."

Again they made the journey up winding stairs. In the topmost storey flames wrapped the wood and glasswork overhead, British snipers redoubled their efforts to dominate the blazing rooms. Axe, bucket and hosepipe were rushed up the numerous ladders leading to the roof. Men plied the axes and hoses with the flames beating pitilessly in their faces, the frequent ping of bullets in their ears, the water which flooded the floors soaking their blood-speckled clothes.

As the hours, which seemed minutes, sped on, the flames roared and leaped, the smoke curled in great clouds, debris crashed in, and the thick concrete floors began to give. The fight against the flames was abandoned as hopeless and the men on the roof were ordered below. Some still obstinately remained long afterwards, firing into the void at the relentless snipers without or struggling gamely against the conquering flames. But now the sheets of flame covered the ground-floor and that above. . . . The upper floors crashed as the men regained the ground-

15

floor and yard. . . . Walls of amber flame, within and without and scaling the walls of stone and leaping over the thunder of the crashing floors, moaning down the shafts to the cellars, where even now bodies of Volunteers were dashing with cases of bombs, armfuls, bucketfuls, sackfuls of grenades, gelignite and other explosives.

Plunkett and Pearse marched round, calling the men to attention in ringing tones. One by one the companies marched into what had been the hospital and secured rations. Cheese and bread were served out, and the men packed as much as possible into their haversacks and knapsacks. Pearse spoke again in the desolate and flaming room: "We are going to fight our way through Moore Street to another position and join forces with the men in the Four Courts." It was rumoured that troops were advancing through the ruins of the Imperial Hotel, now a surly smoking shell facing the burning Headquarters. Snipers would hold them—BANG! Near Macken a tall, dark, broad-shouldered man collapsed, face pallid, eyes closed, a moan escaping from his lips. A shot-gun, held carelessly, had emptied its contents into his back. The orders were completed, and the men filed off in retreat down a passage towards a side-door opening into Henry Street. BANG! A second wounded and moaning figure on the floor.

"Unload and hold your guns up!" came the officers' angry orders. Volunteer stretcher bearers rushed forward, the side-doors swung open, and under Red Cross flags the wounded disappeared into the open. A sound of rifles and machine-guns broke suddenly, nearer and nearer. . . . Inside the flames howled and glowed. . . . Above, through the smoke, the sky showed, and three sculptured figures on the building's front. . . .

"If we escape from this hell-trap," said Macken, pointing to the crevices in the walls, and the blank and fiery street without, "we'll escape from anywhere."

"Throw off your top-coats, lads." said Michael Collins as a volley roared outside, and the red glare silhouetted his shadow on the wall, giant and grotesque. "And blow the devil out of anyone who stops you!"

"Load up!" came the order, and into the glare and turmoil the men dashed at the double. Down laneways into stables, past alleys where machine-guns rattle and flash in the sombre murk, the retreat continues. Bullets pattered on the cobble-stones and walls. Every now and then a man spins round and drops or staggers on, bloody and groaning. Officers rally the men through the fire-swept area with ringing cries and pistols

16

which snap at the hostile darkness, and the deadly marksmen speckling the ranks of the Volunteers with limping and reeling figures.

Another sound is added to the din: picks, spades, pokers, boring and smashing through the walls of houses—a labour which only stops with daylight. The corpses lie on the pavements. The moan and glare of the flames deepen in the blackening night. An officer is carried into a house. He has been riddled within a few hundred yards of a machine-gun. Waxen and eviscerated, he lies in a corner, his dark hair standing dishevelled above his shocked features. Hurling a pick to the floor, Michael Collins dashed up and looked down on the body in silence. It was The O'Rahilly. As a sheet was placed over the body, Sean MacDermott limped from the shadows, a stoic and gentle-eyed mourner.

"Great man, that!" said Michael Collins.

"Yes," said MacDermott. "He knew nothing of our plans until we were on the eve of action. Then he opposed. But he stuck to us, although we implored him to go and told him that would be no dishonour."

A shade of horror darkened Michael Collins's face. He asked brusquely:

"Any other news?"

"Nothing except that there is an armed cordon all round the area. We'll hardly break through. We have had no news from outside since this morning, Thursday. All the main positions were then holding out. We can do little else but hide till daylight."

Behind, a muffled roar swelled to thunder: the explosives in the cellars of the Post Office had been reached by the fires. Hour by hour, Macken and Harding looked through a barricaded window at Nelson's Pillar: the lofty column and the figure on its summit came to a flame-lit life beside the howling furnace. . . . The darkness lifted, and snipers at work away in the city aroused the fitful sleepers.

All day the Volunteers worked feverishly, barricading and reconnoitring the position, piling furniture against the windows or hurling obstructions down stairways to block passages or nailing planks against fragile doors. Groups of scouts crept into the streets and scanned the British barricades in the distance. Sean Condron headed a sortie and stole with Macken and Harding towards a deserted cart and pile of barrels which had served as a barricade earlier in the week. In the shadow of walls they approached closer and closer. . . . Condron

17

groaned softly from time to time, the ache of the shoulder wound he had received during the retreat of the night before. . . . As they reached the barricade, they saw that the street was closed by a stout timber erection, strengthened by sandbags. They watched, but saw no sign of life behind. Condron stood up, and looked more closely. . . . Suddenly, the air was alive with bullets hissing. . . . Tap-tap-tap. . . . A machine-gun played on the cart and barrels. . . . A volley in reply, and the Volunteers dashed back, the barricade in a splintered ruin behind. Macken asked: "Where's Condron?"

"Down there," answered a Volunteer wearily, "with the five others we have lost."

"I don't believe it," said Harding, and taking a curt nod from Macken for assent, he went again towards the shattered cart and barrels in the cover of the walls. There he saw five huddled bodies on the stones—and Sean Condron lying still. The sight left his calloused emotions unstirred. Fear he had, but he was too tired to know it. In the heads of the waxen Volunteers he saw grim red stars, but Condron seemed asleep. He glanced down the still street and saw another waxen corpse in khaki. . . . . A revulsion came over him. . . . How long would all these corpses lie rotting there? . . . Condron moved, and, forgetting all else, Harding rushed to him and carried him quickly away. He reached the houses in silence, and laid the unconscious Condron on the floor. Only then did he realise that the khaki watchers had withheld their fire.

"We're quits now," Macken commented. "Dick Blake heard a poor devil of a Tommy howling on the cobbles in the small hours, and carried him in. He's above in bed in the Head-quarters room now."

Up the stairs to a small bedroom with the unconscious Condron. A khaki figure with the R.A.M.C. badge came forward. He was a prisoner and working overtime on his wounded captors. He shrugged his shoulders and told Harding that Condron had fainted, another small flesh wound. . . . Back to the main body, lying on the floor and staring at the irregular gaping holes in the tunnelled walls of each room. . . .

The snipers continued, and that now remote music of death amid the slates and chimneys of Dublin was the only sound which broke in on the whispers of the listless Volunteers. In a corner, Harding, Macken and Michael Collins sat together in silence. At last Macken spoke—a cynical expression in his heavy eyes:

"Not long to wait now. If the majority of Dublin citizens

could lay hands on us, they'd tear us to pieces. They won't like us walking through their happy homes with pickaxes. But we've had a run for our money all the same."

Michael Collins did not reply. He looked in front of him, abstracted.

An officer beckoned to the three men. They went, rifles in hand, through walls and down stairways until they reached a warehouse yard opening on to the end of Moore Street. . . . From behind a half-tumbled wall they caught sight of a barricade, and khaki sentries and machine-guns waiting, two hundred yards away. In twos and threes more and more Volunteers stole up silently. A halt was called, and the men knew that at a word they must charge into the open. A hopeless task, a counsel of despair, a wave to wear down a rock. . . . The group was fifty strong now, gripping rifles, fixing bayonets, grasping rude bombs —advance guard to create a desperate diversion. They rested and knew few of them could ever reach the barricade alive. . . .

"A third of our force. Yes, I've counted twice," whispered Macken. "Shows we're cornered. As a surprise we might manage it, but here in broad daylight—it's the starkest piece of lunacy in this stark-mad week. And the moment they realise our strength, the game is up. For they could easily overwhelm us or, even more simply, burn us out. So here goes, boys. The last run for our money."

They could see the shattered cart and the dead Volunteers who had fallen in the earlier sortie, and the corpses along the side walk. A wave of pity and disgust passed over Harding, but that he would soon lie there too never troubled his thoughts— trivial things went through his mind, and a half-conscious fear and a wish for rest. A man with the aspect of a benign eagle passed by, a pistol clenched in his hand. He looked into the street, smiled thoughtfully and shook his head. He whispered to a group of officers and went back towards the houses.

"Tom Clarke!" whispered Michael Collins.

Sixteen years in prison and still going strong. . . . Facing his last stone wall. . . .

All at once a deafening volley and burst of machine-gun fire zip-zipped and tap-tapped from the barricade, sweeping the remains of the crazy barrels and riddled cart in the centre of the street before them. Three civilians had dashed from a house and tore madly down the street. . . . Looters, perhaps, hoping to escape into a by-lane, or starving citizens, who could stand hunger no longer. The civilians fell on the cobbles, and writhed into an unobtrusive stillness. . . .

Tom Clarke appeared for a moment at the end of the yard, and shook his head. . . . A murmur ran through the waiting men . . . their officers whispered an order to retire . . . the attack had been postponed until dark. . . . The Volunteers went back and lay again along the floors. Odd volleying and sporadic tap-tapping and the crack of a lone sniper afar off came with mournful echoes through the drab and grey windows—whispers of defeat to an army on the eve of a last stand.

"Until dark, postponed six hours!" muttered Macken. "Six centuries would be nearer the mark. We are sealed in."

Michael Collins sat in a corner, a look of horror in his eyes, a pallor spreading over his face. Disjointed words told Harding that The O'Rahilly's eviscerated corpse and the riddled civilians on the blood-clogged cobbles had come to life in one man's imagination, straining his control to breaking point. Moans escaped him, and he huddled into his corner at every far-away sound. Macken went swiftly to Michael Collins and spoke to him in cheerful undertones. . . . Collins looked up, and his face cleared while his waking nightmare passed. He lay back, stoical and impassive, with the rest of the doomed Volunteers waiting for the end.

CHAPTER II

As Winifred Considine walked through the empty streets and looked back at the tricolours over the Post Office for the last time, she knew that the Rising's hours were numbered. She went ahead in a dream, avoiding a military barrier here, a dangerous lane-way there, sprawling corpses yonder—turning and twisting down the by-ways Sean Condron had sketched for her, after he had told her where Dermott had hidden the plans. . . . And the fatal documents which would tell raiding parties too much when Havensfield was searched. She had left when Pearse was speaking and his burning words were filling the vastness of the lower room. She must visit Agnes MacGowan, and reclaim the bicycle she had left there on Easter Monday. Then, thanks to Sean Condron's careful map of the backways to the Dublin hills, she might undo the damage that Dermott's lapse of memory threatened to cause . . . a hundred names . . . plans. . . . A crash of rifles from the city's centre, a fall of glass, a scream.

She hurried on alone with her thoughts. A phrase linked

itself with tumbled heaps of brick and fire-wreathed shells in O'Connell Street, a phrase which had caught her ear when the flames had glared in and masonry crashed beyond, and Angus Fitzsimmons had distributed the food with careful hand and caustic tongue: a dialogue between Tom Hughes and Michael Collins.

"Terrible destruction, Mick. . . ."

"Don't worry, you old cod, we'll rebuild it, and the whole city in ten years—if necessary."

"No," Angus contradicted, "not the Dublin we have known."

Immortal Dublin, changeless in spirit through all her wars! Still the mounting ruins, though the Post Office and the Custom House and Trinity College and Dublin Castle reared themselves immune. . . . A bad sign, the women and wounded were being removed as she left . . . Dermott in Kerry . . . bungled landing. . . . A ripple of distant volleys.

Agnes MacGowan's at last. She rang the bell, and Patrick Edward MacGowan came to the door, a dazed look in his eyes. He shook her hand warmly, and they went upstairs. There was a crowd in the book-lined room, an uneasy collection of groups, which talked among themselves—a priest, a bald professor, several poets, women with leaden-circled eyes, a knot of the *literati* with beards and tongues a-wag. . . . Into the room crept the terror, indecision and black gloom of non-insurgent Dublin.

"A mad business! There's been no move in the country parts to help them. They can't hold out. Why didn't they wait?"

"Food is running short in the city, and butter was seven and six a pound today."

"But I tell you I heard the Turks landed at Waterford."

"No, the British at Kingstown, you mean. And there was hot work on the road in."

"Met a mad Sinn Feiner on Monday near Portobello. Ever hear the like of this? My bold orator spun past me like a top. I had heard the first shots, but this regular Hoch der Kaiser Robert Emmet lad, always out in his uniform route-marching and taking Dublin Castle with his lungs, well, he could only career past me, bawling: 'Bullets, b-b-bullets, b-b-bullets! Oh, I can't wait!' "

"A lot of the fire-eaters are safe in the feathers. Or walking round pretending they are dispatch riders."

"Father, here's another rosary we would like you to bless."

"And this one too, Father. No, Father, we are not going down to the Post Office. If there was the ghost of a chance,

21

we should be the first to go out with the lads. But the rosaries are a great consolation, Father."

Agnes MacGowan was watching the forest of chimney-pots from the windows, the forest which hid Dublin's heart from her view. . . . Sometimes there was a movement of crowds in the street or the long screaming wail of some sniper in his death agony or cracks and flashes over the roofs. . . . Agnes MacGowan looked up and spoke, oblivious of her surroundings:

'I WISH I WAS DOWN THERE!"

She resumed her watch, and over the city roofs again swept the duel of sniper and machine-gun. Winifred turned to leave the scene, for she suddenly saw the British cordons closing and the planks of barricades falling into position and the challenge of sentries halting her path to Havensfield, already raided ere now perhaps. . . . Patrick Edward MacGowan argued with her as she went down the steps. . . . But she refused his offer to accompany her and told him she must take the chance. . . . Alone she might get through. . . . An escort would attract attention. . . . Men's lives hung on her risk, and she alone must see the documents.

A phantom-haunted ride to Havensfield. She encountered only one military barrier. Some casual questions and the sentry waved her on. Then through groups in the little villages towards where Dublin is fairest with a sky-crown of blunt-topped hills —asparkle from Howth to Killiney with gold, bronze, blue and green shading from emerald to sapphire and agate in the noble and endless mirror of the sea. She speeded inland through a forest of pines traversed by curling roads curving towards the city. Through wide spaces with fleeces of heather and furze, studded with grey moss-speckled boulders over which she had often seen rabbits scamper or wild birds' lingering swoop. Low stone walls crossed over and scaled the neighbouring slopes. From wooded hollows beneath came the sound of bells and voices. In remote fields cattle grazed. Small dark figures shadowed reluctant horses up the mountain slopes. She was in the heart of the hills. The grey walls of Havensfield rose to meet her. Up the winding avenue to an empty house.

To Dermott's room. The click of a panel, and then a blazing heap of oil-drenched letters and plans and documents in a grate. She walked through the silent rooms when she had thrown the ashes on the winds towards Dublin and the flickering sky above it. Tumbled beds where the Volunteers had slept. Silence and desolation and the presage of defeat. She remembered the twenty Volunteers marching down the road when Sean Condron's message had reached them, the talk of the split which had kept half of the men whom Dermott and Condron had drilled in the little mill at home. . . . Well, all their secrets were safe now in spite of all.

Through the upper windows, Dublin lay below, spires and roofs half-hidden in a heat mist five miles away, the restful green, the pines, the elms, the Bay there faintly yonder where the woodlands dipped, then to the city again and the horrific deepening of yellows and scarlets in the skies above it, a whirl of flame and a choir of thunders. It was early evening, and the light just falling.

Winifred looked down the avenue and saw what she had expected to see so often in the years of preparation in the years before Easter Eve: a long line of khaki men marching towards the house. They glanced at every tree for an ambush behind. Havensfield was surrounded. A hammering on the doors. In the fiery clouds above Dublin gusts of smoke sweeping higher and higher. Detonations. BOOM. . . . BOOM. . . . BOOM. . . . To her inward ear the crash of masonry again, and with each dying report the face of a man she knew and his death knell perhaps. . . . Splintering wood. . . . Footsteps. A British officer was speaking to her, and from other rooms came rumours of a furious search.

He was a courteous young man, but persistent. Where were the arms concealed? How many men had slept there? How many rebels were there in the hills? Her name? Where was Dermott Considine? And to each question she answered quietly:

"I don't know, and even if I did I would not tell you."

Dan Hogan, the G-man with his dark hawk eyes, came in and identified her. She looked at them both with bitterness, and said:

"My answer to every question, even to what my name may be, is No! Do you understand?"

The search continued. The raiders found nothing, not even that empty secret room. Nor a scrap of paper. Winifred had seen to that. Dan Hogan found a Japanese sword in the hall and tore it down. An antique horse pistol too and a battered sword-cane Dermott had picked up on the quays. Orders were orders: all lethal weapons. The officer threw them back on a table wearily.

"Lethal weapons!" he said. "Search for rifles, revolvers, bombs, bullets, bayonets, trench-knives and swords with edges, but leave silly toys behind or articles of sentimental value, or kitchen knives or hammers, bows and arrows or household utensils."

When the search ended, and the long line of khaki prepared to march off down the avenue, the officer said simply:

"I do not blame you for not answering my questions. If the cases were reversed, we should not like our women to give us away."

Darkness shot and lighted with blazing, roaring, howling rings and spirals in, from and above the city's core. . . . Louder and louder the noise of the guns swept up to her, and she thought of the words of the father she had never seen and his long years in an English prison and the words her dead mother had told her were always on his lips: "Yes, the power of England is a stone wall, but I will chance an Irish skull against it till one or the other breaks. . . ." And she thought, too, of the grim legacy which had come to the generations of Ireland since Henry II had landed, and Elizabethan and Cromwellian adventurers had shattered the Decalogue for riches nearer than the Spanish Main, and the Gaelic civilization had gone down, and Tone had died and Emmet failed, and O'Donovan Rossa schemed and stormed in his prison cell in vain. A tragic procession of the insurgent leaders of the Irish and the fate which had destroyed their plan in the last hour. Until this last hour, too, when Pearse and Clarke stood below with only 700 men. . . . Pearse's words at O'Donovan Rossa's grave came back:

"Life springs from death; and from the graves of patriot men and women spring living nations. . . . And while Ireland holds these graves, Ireland unfree shall never be at peace."

Tradition, memory and tragedy in the veins of Ireland, women reading dead history in dull books and in due course breaking their hearts over living history in dying men. . . . Dermott, a wandering fugitive in Kerry. . . . Back to the days she had passed in the Post Office, and the war in her mind as she watched the Volunteers waging their unequal fight. She had turned to Harding and said in the main hall: "Even now, I am not sure, not even if the British broke in, whether it is right to take life for any cause. The Volunteers are all right. They can just obey their officers. Better die in Dublin and not in Flanders. But for me——" She weighed the issue again, but no answer came. Yet Pearse was right. Death for the truth is never bitter. . . .

A wave of hope swept through her, impersonal and prophetic, a kindling and fusing of the wisdom of the centuries. Ireland would never be the same again. She had grown greater on her failures. Away in Kerry it would be told for a hundred years, that tale of the night when the arms landing failed, a red light shone over the seas and Roger Casement came. . . .

A sea of flame, higher, higher, higher, and explosions resounding in the night. . . . Great flames where the Post Office had been, one ocean of scarlet. . . . EVERY VOLUNTEER IN DUBLIN WOULD BE BURNED ALIVE. . . . EVERY VOLUNTEER WITHIN THAT SEA OF FIRE WAS BURNING, BURNING, BURNING. . . .

She watched, rigid and tearless, until the sun broke in its glory over elm and pine and woodland and the distant Bay. . . . Only the harvest of tomorrow now, tomorrow mocking hope, too, perhaps. But the war in her mind was for ever stilled.

CHAPTER III

TOWARDS evening a lull, deadly and ominous, descended on Dublin, racked by machine-gun fire and the five days' agony. Only remote snipers broke the silence. O'Connell Street was a smouldering mass of ruins. Through the unnatural calm at long intervals came occasional faint reports. In Moore Street the Volunteers still stared in front of them as they lay along the floors, on beds, around tables—too indifferent to talk, eat or sleep. Through a hole in the wall of the room he had left half an hour before, Michael Collins climbed and shouted to the men that the orders were to rest till nightfall in preparation for any sortie.

He went to the corner where Macken half-dozed, and whispered eagerly.

"Do you know what MacDermott has just told me? The leaders have sent out to negotiate and save the men from slaughter. For that was the phrase Willie Pearse used in the Headquarters room just now: 'For slaughter it is.' And Connolly, they say, stopped staring in front of him, lying wounded in bed, and spoke too: 'I don't care if the men are shot down here, but I won't have them burned.' Still, say nothing yet, for it may come to nothing, and we'll go below to tackle that barricade."

"Wake up, boys!" cried an officer, running through the room. "Good news soon." Then Michael Collins heard a hundred rumours confirm his whisper: UNCONDITIONAL SURRENDER. Down the cheeks of some, tears ran. Others were sullen and angry-eyed. Here and there threats were muttered. Men sprang up and splintered the butts of their rifles against walls and hurled bolts, magazines and ammunition down stairways, snarling.

Sean Condron shouted to the men and checked the destruction. He gave an order to Macken and Harding. They walked through the rooms repeating his question:

"Have you taken anything that does not belong to you? If so, leave it behind. They will only be too glad to call us looters."

But in room after room the Volunteers shook their heads and went back to the fierce discussion of the surrender. At last Harding and Macken met a worried little man with iron-grey hair sitting apart. He had found a comb with a gaudy tinsel back on a mantelpiece, which he had taken as a souvenir for his wife. It was gravely decided that the comb be restored to the mantelpiece, and the worried little man said what matter when they might all be shot, anyway; but it was no use giving those bloody bastards a loophole, for they always slandered their enemies, except the like of Kruger, who stood up to them, when, be Jasus, they craved for mercy; and it had been a great fight, and, be Jasus, it would last a month next time, and it was an answer to the recruiting sergeants, and perhaps the terms might prove more favourable than some feared.

At last the companies all lined up and marched through the ruined walls to a warehouse, where Sean MacDermott read Pearse's message to them, his eyes sombre, but with a hint of tears in his calm and intense gaze, a sudden touch of passion and pride in his voice:

"IN ORDER TO PREVENT THE FURTHER SLAUGHTER OF DUBLIN CITIZENS, AND IN THE HOPE OF SAVING THE LIVES OF OUR FOLLOWERS, NOW SURROUNDED AND HOPELESSLY OUTNUMBERED, THE MEMBERS OF THE PROVISIONAL GOVERNMENT PRESENT AT HEADQUARTERS HAVE AGREED TO AN UNCONDITIONAL SURRENDER, AND THE COMMANDANTS OF THE VARIOUS DISTRICTS IN THE CITY AND COUNTY WILL ORDER THEIR COMMANDS TO LAY DOWN ARMS."

Dead silence followed the reading. Then Sean MacDermott spoke to the men simply, ordering food to be served out to them. His voice trembled with anger as he looked with affection on the haggard groups before him:

"The only terms the British military authorities would listen to were an unconditional surrender. We surrendered not to save you, but the city and the people of this city. But no matter! I am proud of you. . . . It was not your fault that we have not won the Republic. . . . You made a great fight. . . . You were outclassed, that is all. . . . They had the men, the munitions, the force. . . . But this week of Easter will be remembered, and your work will tell some day!"

Out into Moore Street marched the odd few hundred men, variously armed, but still alert with a certain wonder and a certain pride. Slowly, in that ghastly street, strewn with debris, starred with the waxen corpses in khaki and grey-green, some civilians, huddled, ragged and blood-specked, the small band lined up and listened to final instructions. They were to march to the Parnell Monument and lay down their arms. Some, over-wrought, mistook the order for the liberation of the prisoners held by the Volunteers as a sign that they themselves would soon be free. A feeble cheer arose, to be drowned by an angry hiss from the ranks. Sleepless, hungry, wounded, defeated, these men were defiant amidst the crash of all their dreams. White flags fluttered bird-like at their head and rear as with firm and regular step they swung into O'Connell Street, now lined by a forest of khaki and steel. The fires still burned. Above the blackened skeletons of the Imperial Hotel and Post Office tricolours flapped against the April sky.

As the marchers round Henry Street corner two British officers cover each pair of men with enormous revolvers. Arms, knapsacks, equipment are dumped in the centre of the street. A general strides down the lines, his long grey face alight beneath the red band on his cap. He asks if there are any wounded. He tells the prisoners that they will be watered and fed. He vanishes with weary eyes. Second lieutenants fumble with their notebooks and the unusual Irish names. Bluff sergeants swear to send all the Bloody Etceteras to Hell, and quickly, and in a lurid variety of ways. The Tommies, for the most part, watch the ceremony impartially.

Harding looked up at the clear sky and down again at his comrades—a handful in comparison to the deep long lines of khaki. Behind him a Tommy conversed in whispers with Macken and Michael Collins. Was that all there was of them? Well, he reckoned they wouldn't half catch what for. He hadn't slept for two nights and was glad they had stopped. Old Casement had been taken on the Kerry coast and had a bullet put through him. The Tommy added cheerfully:

"Wish to Christ you poor blokes had got more of our officers. A pity, ain't it? The bleeders, 'ark at 'em!"

A few yards away a sergeant was yelling:

"Nice murdering lot of bleeders you are! Thought you could get away with it, did you? Well, you bleeding well can't. See? I've something down the street that'll make marmalade of the 'ole bitching lot of you, you cross-eyed bastards and bandy-legged sons of bitches! Make me ashamed of being a bleeding Irishman you do. Just you bleeding well wait. I shan't be ashamed bleeding long! See?"

"The language of these fellows!" sighed Dick Blake virtuously. "Showing what they are!"

An officer strode down upon the sergeant with an admonishing roar:

"Come away and don't talk to those damned rebels! You behind there! Don't leave down those rifles! There's still fighting going on in Dublin!"

Down the line came several figures in khaki, lieutenants taking down names and addresses, while from the front a voice thundered:

"No fictitious names and addresses, or the consequences will be serious." Red Cross wagons hummed and glided up and down the street. The Volunteers glowered as the arms were borne away from where they had dumped them. Nearer and nearer to Harding and Macken came a khaki figure and its notebook. Then they both started:

"Names, please?"

Terence O'Donovan stood before them. He noted their names, smiling to himself. . . . Old arguments in the days before Terence had left for Flanders. . . . Pensive, a gonfalon for ever in his eyes, so deep and smouldering, a force in the straight and pugnacious nose. . . .

"You are the real sort," said Terence O'Donovan. "You ought to have stars after your names. Why the devil couldn't you wait till the war stopped, anyway?"

"Thought you were killed!" said Macken. "Haven't heard a word of you since the night of the O'Donovan Rossa funeral, when you and Bernard and the rest of us had the argument in the pub. Two years since you joined up. You look fit. You must love war."

"Heard you were missing," said Harding. "We soon may be."

"We knocked the lard out of your crowd," said Dick Blake, giving his name. "Haven't you the Germans licked yet?"

"All in good time. No romantic suicide for me," said Terence O'Donovan. "Tear up any compromising documents you have and throw them behind you. Dangerous times. Wigs on the green!"

"Who's that old stick?" asked Michael Collins before Terence had disappeared from sight. "I met him somewhere with you, I think."

"Yes," said Macken. "Didn't you hear me? The night of the Rossa funeral, in Tom O'Dea's pub behind the Custom House. Bernard was there, and Harding here and two other reporters, Kerrigan of the *Emancipator* and Bolger of the *Liberator*."

"Now I remember," said Michael Collins. "He had a dry ginger, and Bernard and Kerrigan nearly came to blows over the Irish Party and the history of the *Emancipator*."

"Aye," said Dick Blake. "Then Bolger broke in with the eternal topic, all the women he has slept with, and *we* broke up in disorder. Mind you, Bernard was a bit of a holy boy; the Lord have mercy on him."

"If he was as great a saint as Bolger is a liar," said Macken, "he's playing a harp now."

"Jasus," said Dick Blake, "perhaps we'll soon join him."

"Touch wood, you gouger!" said Michael Collins, looking grimly in front of him. Harding looked at Collins sideways, and from that moment something of a spell fell over him. What was there in this man that marked him out from the crowd? A curious fancy came into Harding's brain, and he smiled at the contrast as he watched the peaceful sky darken, and more and more parties of Volunteers marched into the street, small dwarfish knots in the khaki lines stretching from the Parnell Monument to Earl Street. Back went Harding's memory to the night of the O'Donovan Rossa funeral, and a small yellow book in his pocket: *Bedach An Chota Lachtna*, "The Churl of the Drab Coat." . . . The warrior who came to the fabled Gaels of old when the King of Thessaly's son had demanded tribute and overlordship . . . swilled a hogshead of wine at a gulp and wolfed his fill of flesh. . . . Darker grew the sky and his own mood . . . shouting voices . . . grey parties in the darkening street. . . . Michael Collins in the ranks darkly brooding. . . . Gaelic letters flashing in Harding's eyes, while the shouting died away and a torch flashed behind them and threw a gaunt and grotesque shadow on the cobbles in front of them—the gaunt and grotesque shadow of Michael Collins—and through Harding's restless brain passed the closing words of the old heroic tale:

"An awesome Spectre, forbidding in looks, a Fearsome One, like a ferocious Devil-Giant, Fionn saw, and he going through the tangled and gloomy wood. . . . A Drab Coat was wrapped about him with mud-beplastered skirts, his tremendous brogues thundering like mighty waves every pace he strode. . . . But when the Churl of the Drab Coat came from the ship to the place where Fionn and his warriors stood, lo! the wind and the sun flamed before and behind, and they saw then 'twas MANANNAN MAC LIR, Fairy Phantom of Rathcroghan, who had come to save them in the dire strait in which they were."

Sharp commands sounded abruptly, and to a grass plot before the Rotunda Hospital the prisoners were marched, rank and file, Cumann na mBan girls, leaders, and herded there amidst a circle of bayonets. On the roofs a party of snipers and machine-gunners kept vigil. A broad-browed, dark-faced, thick-lipped captain in khaki arrived, perhaps crazy, perhaps drunk, perhaps just a bully flushed with power. He stamped round shouting, and the more he shouted the more a brogue emerged to clash with the accent he had learned in the wars, but in the plainest Anglo-Saxon—brogue or no brogue—and in megaphone tones he howled his edicts: no one must stand up, no one must sit down, and as to the ordinary needs of nature, people who chose gardens for beds could use them for lavatories as well and jolly well lie in both. A mechanical chorus answered his questions to the relief arriving:

"Which are the worst, the Sinn Feiners or the Germans?"

"The Sinn Feiners!" droned the guard.

"What shall we do with them?"

"Shoot 'em!"

The night passed on, and the heaped-up, hatless, coatless mass of prisoners had broken dreams with glimpses of an upright circle of bayonets and the rigid faces of the guard behind.

Heavily escorted, the Volunteers marched away on Sunday morning to Richmond Barracks through empty and sometimes smouldering streets. In the main thoroughfares angry voices yelled to temerarious onlookers in the upper storeys of the houses which lined the route to close the windows. Staff officers shouted to the Tommies to watch their rifles and understand that all the rebel positions had not surrendered yet. Into the great yard of the barracks, where, amidst grounding of rifles and more shouting, there was a general halt. The Tommies held out their water-bottles to the thirsty prisoners. A staff officer, trembling with excitement, ordered them back. A sergeant spat on the ground as he obeyed.

"Men are men," he muttered in reply to a question from the Tommies. "Even if they do pick you off from behind the chimney-pots!"

Then forward into the barrack rooms, with their gloomy windows and stinking slop buckets. A crowd of detectives, sleek and keen-eyed, accompanied by staff officers, moved among

30

the prisoners—gloating, truculent, hovering, pouncing. One in particular struck Harding's imagination: Dan Hogan, with his drooping black moustache, bowler hat, six feet and greedy eyes. Chuckling, he pointed and pounced, and pointed and pounced again. Soon a long row of the men he had identified were ranged along a wall. Michael Collins in the ranks brooded still, his jaw set and in his eyes a light as remorseless as that in Dan Hogan's.

Two detectives swooped suddenly on Harding and Macken and hurried them out of the room. Then, when they had hustled their captures into another room, both detectives laughed loudly and said to each other:

"That's one for the bastard. Wonder he didn't spot these lads before."

"Hello, David," said the first detective, winking. "You had better stay here. Dan Hogan's on the job, and he's too obliging to his red-hatted pals. He's after the big fish for the moment, but he'll begin to work his memory and think of all the lads he spotted on the route marches. I remember all your little pars in the *Emancipator*. But keep your mouth shut, young fellow. A nod is as good as a wink!"

"I knew you well, Mr. Macken!" the second detective was saying. "Didn't you wire my sister-in-law's house, and a damned fine job you made of it. Let the pair of you say you were caught in the row by accident and we'll get you out. A tradesman and a journalist, nothing easier."

"No damned fear!" snapped Macken.

"We'll take our chance with the rest," said Harding.

"Well, good luck," said the detective. "You are a mad collection, you fellows. The quietest country in the world, and Home Rule and his own porter barrel coming to every man of us after the war if you'd only sat snug and tight."

"Good-bye, boys," said the second. "If they get you, it won't be long before they get us. It'd be an ill day for us when we'd help yon crowd against our own countrymen. But things are blue, shocking blue!"

Soon the door opened and other Volunteers were pushed in. The room filled. Dick Blake came in. The identification parade continued. Dan Hogan hovered round group after group. Sergeants peered in and shouted for those under sixteen to step forward for release as under age. The Volunteers waited stoically, wondering what had happened outside Dublin, how their relatives fared and when the long procession would cease. Hogan pounced at intervals. Once the room rose with a menacing hiss as he badgered a youth of pale and quiet mien with questions: Where had he got the coat he was wearing? What did he know of the whereabouts of the man beside him during Easter Week? What had he whispered to him about guns just now?

"He's my father, you spying dirt-bird!" shrieked the youth all at once. "And perhaps you'll meet a man and a stick in a dark lane some dark night that'll make you sorry and sore?"

" 'Ere, enough of this!" interrupted a sergeant, hurrying Hogan out. Three Tommies with blank expressions came in and shook their heads solemnly. No, they had not seen any of these men in the Post Office. . . . Nor fighting anywhere else during the week. . . . As they left the room, they turned and winked good-naturedly.

A second lieutenant with keen gaze entered and peered into the face of Volunteer after Volunteer. He joked, and they laughed bitterly. "Oh, yes, you Irish want a Republic. Well, you simply can't have it!" He pointed suddenly, and a Volunteer officer with a Red Cross armlet was led away. "I'll never forget your face!" said the lieutenant sharply. "You held me up in the street outside the Post Office with a revolver. But I was not sure till I saw the gold filling in your teeth!"

Dick Blake sat up and swore lustily.

"The little squirt! If yon lad captured him, didn't he save his bloody life twice? When he took him in out of harm's way, and when he remembered he had been locked up in the blazing cellars after the fires took place, and went down at the risk of his life to rescue him?"

Macken laughed.

"He thinks he's doing his duty, Dick. Didn't you notice the Tommies winking at us time and again today?"

"What do you think they'll do with us, Arthur?"

"Not much! They can only shoot us or lock us up, anyway!"

Again the door opened, and a party of Tommies appeared, dragging a sooty and dishevelled man between them. They flung him into the room with a shout:

"Here's your bleeding general! Found him up a chimney. Hiding. Good-bye. Short-arm inspection later!"

A sergeant came in and served out tins of bully beef and biscuits from a large bucket with the cheery advice:

"Tuck in and help yourselves, my lads, for you might just as well be shot on full bellies as on empty ones!"

At evening Macken and his comrades found themselves again in the barrack yard, a forest of bayonets around them and overhead the gentle spring sky. As they lined up to march away,

Harding noticed Sean MacDermott limping beside Michael Collins.

"Stop!" cried a loud and eager voice, and Dan Hogan swooped. "We want that man. He's one of the most dangerous men in Dublin. He signed the Proclamation." Sean MacDermott was led inside again, and Michael Collins looked after him with a grim look.

Along the quaysides, then past the rude dismantled barricades, smoking ruins and human litter putrefying on the pavements. A drunken woman reeled from a side-lane, waving a cabbage stalk as they neared the North Wall. "Fools, fools that yous were!" she shrilled. "Yous might as well have tried to fight the Government with a pitch-fork!" Then she twirled her skirts high, screaming: "That to you, you khaki cut-throats!"

"Go 'ome, mother!" said the Tommies, grinning.

As they reached the cattle-boat, Harding looked back at Dublin, the Custom House, the handsome buildings behind, and said:

"We can't be too bad, after all. They had to throw us out!"

"Too bad! The Five Days!" answered Macken. "Better than Ninety-Eight!"

Beneath them, all huddled on life-belts down in the stinking hold, bubbled the waters of the Irish Sea. They fell into nightmare dozings until Holyhead rose before them in a clear and cloudless dawn. They did not know whether they would ever see Ireland again, whether they were going to imprisonment or death. In their hearts a pride stirred and a feeling that somehow their deed would not be in vain, even though a white flag flew above the ruin of their dream.

CHAPTER IV

BRICKS, bricks, bricks, a black iron door and thirty-five panes of glass. Backwards and forwards. Round and round. Absolute isolation: no news, no conversation, no books, no one even to look at. And the outside world belonged to the past. Time reduced to the shadow of the sunlight on the high brick wall opposite, and visible through one, two, three, yes, five, ten, fifteen, twenty, twenty-five, thirty, thirty-five panes of glass. Over the wall stole the distant noises of the little English town, the cries of the sentries for a lullaby when tea, brown, rich, deep, huge chunk of bread, had been served at half-past four on a bright summer evening; the sergeant with the prying eyes and flaming visage, a Roman Catholic himself because his sister kept a pub at the North Wall, Dublin, clicking the spy-hole. To dream, weary brain. To dream wild and mixed dreams and wonder what had happened, perhaps, a month ago, perhaps a week or century ago in Dublin and outside Dublin. . . . Was the Great War still going on, that curious Verdun battle? . . . Had the country beyond Dublin risen? . . . Had the leaders been shot? . . . Considine in Kerry . . . bungled landing . . . could he escape . . . little mill . . . Dermott holding them together there after Redmond had made the recruiting speech and the split came. . . . Tiger Doyle drilled there. . . . Dermott Considine's nerve broke, some said. . . . HUNGER! Was there anything so real in life as food, bread and those crumbs that fell on the doorstep when the bread was handed in this morning? . . . Bombs bursting and rifles rattling in the cell next door, however could so many things be packed into one small cell, ah, the walls were down, that was why. BOOM, BOOM, BOOM! cheese, huge rounds of cheese, that poet chap, Thomas MacDonagh who signed the Proclamation, walking down Camden Street talking excitedly to a British officer just as he did at Howth and Bernard, and the rest got away over the fields, no not an officer, Castle official, no matter the officer was near listening, talking excitedly in Camden Street, laughing and joking then, what's the matter, are we in England or Ireland? Why think about Thomas MacDonagh? Young lad in train from Holyhead who had been in Jacob's fighting under MacDonagh must have said something. Whole carriage talking. Didn't know what we were in for. Do the same again. Richmond Red Hats delighted for they had bagged the whole Sinn Fein movement. Lock us up now and we will not come out for another ten years or so like the Fenians. Lad from Jacob's in a house towards the end of the week. Captain wounded. Cut off. Ten men agree to fight to a finish. Priest comes out and speaks to them: "For the sake of God, men, and the women and children, listen to me. You don't know what we've endured for the past week. I ask you to call a truce so that the wounded and dead may be taken off the streets! The English have called a truce." Dark fellow there wanted to fight to a finish. Had walked in the lad said at the last moment. TIGER DOYLE. What had Mick said? First the Tiger had funked it. Dead brother. That was the seed of war. Shooting brothers. Casement dead on the Kerry coast. Leaders shot? It would all start again when we get out in ten or twenty years like the Fenians and Tom Clarke. Milroy falling flat in

34

a heap, stiff and two jagged wounds in his head
didn't he, why did he? Bernard that sort of m:
the dark of the cell, apt scriptural phrase "Terro
callous then in the street with the five red star
heads, reaction now, forgotten we were afra
numb when up against it, everyone was afraid .
it, the Volunteers, the Tommies and the Red Hats were afraid,
only liars and fools don't duck bullets, talking, dozing, feasts of
bread and cheese and oceans of tea:

GET UP! GAWD LOVE YER!

Another day and another night. Backwards and forwards.
Round and round. One, two, three, four, five, ten, fifteen,
twenty, twenty-five, thirty, thirty-five panes of glass. It would
go on for ever. Nearly three weeks in solitary confinement.
Kept a note of that on the slate.

David Harding strode round and round his cell. He had
grown a young beard and he had stopped thinking. He ate
savagely and gulped the cocoa before him. Every morning the
cell doors were opened separately to prevent the prisoners see-
ing those on the opposite landings. An hour and a half's exercise walking round and round the stone-lined yards below.
Round and round a series of geometrical monstrosities—a joy-
less relaxation, three paces apart, walking, doubling, trotting
while sergeants and lance-corporals posed, statuesque, on stone
eminences. Outside a guardroom near the entrance soldiers and
sometimes a lieutenant or two sprawled and stared. No talking!

Back to the cell with black-iron door, vistas of bricks, grey
beflagged floor, and window with thirty-five panes of glass.

FOOD. Noon and a hash of soup, beans and thready meat
in a tin, and bread. More appetising than all the feasts in the
Arabian Nights, understand how the animals in the Zoo must
feel, bring nuts to the monkeys if ever we get out of this, and
go out too, and cram full of cheese and beef and bread till we
burst, and start all over again. . . .

Silence everywhere except shouts or a whistle at rare intervals
from the bottom of the jail:

WAIT, MY LOVE, AND I'LL BE WITH YOU!

Every evening at the same time that lad lets fly. Bless him,
how he cheers us up! Trust a Dublin man to find fun in Hell
itself! Now for the sergeant with the foghorn throat:

STOP THAT DAMNED WHISTLING DOWN THERE!

Now for the lad, he never misses:

WAITING ROUND THE CORNER!

Tea and bread. Civilian subordinates, blue-coated, greasy and

35

ot-nosed, glide on rubber soles to the spy-holes, smiting the
ors and yelling to those still wakeful to put their beds down.
Down! Then the sentries' cry, the fading light, the clang of rifles
grounding, and sleep. . . . Bricks, bricks, bricks, a black-iron
door and thirty-five panes of glass . . . Never see the streets of
Dublin again. . . . White flags . . . blood . . . cigar smoke . . .
caverns dark of dreams . . . Winifred Considine's face . . . shrine
of all the beauty of the earth. . . . Tomorrow, backwards and
forwards. Round and round. . . .

     .   .   .   .   .   .

Through the isolation mixed tidings broke. Sometimes the
orderlies brought a whisper with the morning slop pails or as
they later slid the bread basket along the shining rails of the
landings. Or a whisper passed in the chapel on Sundays. Or
code messages tapped through the walls, brief and somewhat
incoherent.

Then a talk with a sentry through the window:

"Lucky blighters, you inside—have your dinner, no standing
in the wet. Had you machine-guns in Dublin? Where did you
get them? Even if you did want Home Rule, why didn't you
wait till the war was over, when the military wouldn't have so
much on their hands? Silly old bleeder down the town says
you all ought to be shot. Sergeant Jolly, bloke in charge of
your landing—mad Irishman himself—told him to go and fight
for his own bleeding country half as well as you poor bleeders.
Don't know Sergeant Jolly? 'E 'ates Carson! Proper Socialist!"

In the third week the world came nearer as they filed into the
small chapel, and notes and whispers passed. Volunteer orderlies took the place of the soldier prisoners, and whispers of a
change came three times a day. . . . Asquith in Dublin. . . .
Provisional Government for Ireland . . . release soon . . . after
the war.

One evening Harding had fallen half-asleep when the door
opened and a sergeant entered. A Dublin drill hall in 1913, a
roar and a chuckle, an ex-Army sergeant putting the Volunteers
through their paces while Bernard Milroy glowered and Sean
Condron winked. Herbert Edward Jolly, no other than he, who
had drilled the lads the I.R.B. had drilled on the quiet before
the Volunteers started, and wondered why he could lick them
into shape so quick, marching round the hall with Sean Condron
winking and patting himself on the back.

"Well, my lad, I'm in charge of this landing now. 'Ow did
you get into this mess?"

"Through what you taught me in Parnell Square, Dublin, in 1913!"

"Another of you! Well, I'm blowed! You blokes are all over the shop. Mighty quick in the uptake. Wish the young recruits were half as lively. If you had to go in the Army, maybe you wouldn't be so anxious!"

Back from the wars was Herbert Edward Jolly, and minus an eye, or rather plus a glass one. Oh, yes, he'd left that one in the Dardanelles, and had been sent home on a transport, and some people had thought they had a canary to feed on that little trip. He went on:

"Why didn't you wait till the war was over? I'd 'ave 'elped you then. Nice mess now. Pearse, Connolly and fifteen of your best men shot. Dublin in ruins. But don't you worry. They can't lay a finger on you fellows. No, not a finger if you speak up to them and tell them straight that you thought you was going out to fight Carson and the aristocracy!"

Sergeant Jolly turned to go, but asked suddenly:

"Do you know old Mick Collins? Oh, he's a card, he is. That there sergeant-major tried to tell 'im off last week, and crikey, he came off second best. Then he went next door where Dick Blake is and tried to take it out of 'im, and there 'e learned words 'e never heard before. Lot of old friends in this wing. Gives me the creeps to watch 'em through the spy-'ole. Weeping some of 'em. More fit to be tied and walking round on their 'eads. A poet blew in last week who said 'e started the 'ole business. Considine they call 'im. So we didn't take no chances, but shoved 'im into a cell all to 'isself with a china teapot. Then there's the Tiger Doyle who came over on the same boat. Won't say nothing to nobody. Good night. The worst is over now. You blokes are going to 'ave political treatment. Then they'll shove you up to a camp in Wales till the war stops, and you and that there Carson can 'ave it out till you're blue in the face."

· · · · · ·

Harding sat on his bed till dawn surprised him. Tears upstarted when he recalled those who had fallen. The memory would haunt Ireland until those ghosts were laid. "The fools, the fools, the fools, they have left us our Fenian dead . . . and Ireland unfree will never be at peace." Pearse's words at O'Donovan Rossa's grave. And Pearse was gone. . . . And Tom Clarke too, who had dreamed for sixteen years in prison of the Five Days. . . . New legacies of hate . . . Ireland would rise in anger sooner or later over the newer graves. . . . A new

movement? The Great War? . . . All over the world ghosts
and hatreds pressed all magic and beauty from the sap of life.
. . . Onwards in curious thought meanderings through gnawing
heartaches and doubts to a June morning.

And with that morning the cell doors were thrown open and
all barriers to human intercourse vanished to the click of
Sergeant Jolly's keys. Along the landings the prisoners tramped
to the exercise yard and saw the world again.

Dick Blake sat near the iron railings and sang a popular ditty,
a minute epic of his woes and wants in solitary confinement:

> *Now in this jail we're lodging for being crusty with the King!*
> *Tooralooral, looral, ooraley!*
> *One hour a day for exercise, all walking in a ring.*
> *Tooralooral, looral ooraley!*

Then Dick looked up and said:

"We had visitors from Dublin this morning. My little daughter
May managed the trip. We had a long chin wag at the gate, and
Sergeant Jolly turned his back at the right moment, and she
slipped me this song the kids are singing in Dublin now, and
what the chistlers sing there is always a sign the way the wind
is blowing. Now, listen here:

> *Who fears to speak of Easter Week?*
> *Who dares its fate deplore?*
> *The red-gold flame of Erin's name*
> *Confronts the world once more.*
> *So, Irishmen, remember then*
> *And lift your heads with pride,*
> *For great men and straight men*
> *Have fought for you and died.*

Arthur Macken smiled, lean and bewhiskered and a new fire
in his eyes. The new song thrilled and pleased him. Then the
old mocking expression came back into his face. He changed
his tone and said with a cynical grin:

"Sing the last verse, Dick. It's about us."

"Ah, what are you always jeering at, Arthur? It's a fine verse
all right. Here goes. Glad there's someone to speak up for us."

Dick Blake's voice again rolled out, and a small crowd
gathered round him, humming the closing words:

> *The brave who've gone to linger on,*
> *Beneath the tyrant's heel,*
> *We know they'll pray another day*
> *With clang of clashing steel.*

And from their cells their voices swell
And loudly call on you,
To ask, men, the task, men,
That yet remains to do.

Silent in the growing group stood Michael Collins. Thinner
and more reserved he seemed that morning. His grey-blue eyes
danced and he laughed with a simple delight. Then, with a
boisterous oath, he dashed away to where a rude and violent
contest called by courtesy a football match was in progress.
Towards the centre of the exercise ground darted Michael
Collins whooping. A wave and then another wave of shouting
humans flowed together, and fell in plunging and roaring heaps
on a make-shift paper ball. Michael Collins hurled himself left
and right until the human sea caught and buried him beneath.
. . . Then he emerged again whooping with wild relief. Sergeant
Jolly crossed the yard, exclaiming aloud:

"That there Mick Collins. Oh, he's a proper card, he is!
Just wait till he meets the Red Hats behind the barbed wire
that's waiting for 'im. 'E'll go mad, he will!"

.   .   .   .   .   .

Frongoch Internment Camp in the midst of the bracing air,
the hills and valleys of North Wales. There were two camps,
North and South. The South Camp was a disused distillery,
divided into three parts: the building proper, yards and buildings
adjoining, and a big field. Sentries with shot-guns were stationed
on hutches without. A tall red-brick chimney dominated all,
soaring above the endless intricacies of wire, wood and stone.
Beyond, high hills and stretches of woods and greenlands. Outside the barbed wire, the soldiers' quarters and long white
country roads running between both camps. The North Camp
was a collection of wooden huts and a wired-in field.

The shrill hooter sounded every morning and the hundreds
of men in the barn-like dormitories rolled from their military
blankets and hurried to be counted in rows of four and all
stages of dress and undress. All Ireland was there, a strange
new Ireland reborn in the Easter fires, leaderless, restless, but
dimly aware that nothing would be again as of old. Hundreds
of men, with fine wrinkles round the eyes of all, an easy strained
expression, watching the iron gate until an officer and a Welsh
sergeant came through it to conduct the count. The hooter
moans and screams. All Ireland listens, every grade and type
of Ireland, urban, rural, exiled, home-staying sane, mad, non-

39

descript, in the diverse garbs of Ireland, with Ireland's many accents. . . .

Into the warehouse stream the hundreds of men when the count is finished—into the long rooms flanked with shower baths, rousing and violent, tables down the centre with iron pipes running lengthwise and brass taps attached. There is a channel down the centre of each table along which the water splashes into runnels below.

Breakfast in the huts at seven-thirty in an emigrant-ship atmosphere amidst a great din. Twenty-two tables with folding seats. Eight-thirty, and the hundreds divide into fatigue parties. Or go off to the field to walk round, lie down on the damp or scorching grass. . . . At eleven the hooter wails and screams again. The British Commandant has finished his rounds and calls out to the prisoners:

"Good morning!"

Noon, dinner; field again from two-thirty till four-thirty; tea, five-thirty; freedom comparative until eight-thirty, when the British Commandant, accompanied by the little Welsh sergeant, again inspects and counts.

Then the hundreds drink strong tea in enamel mugs and talk till all the lights are switched off in the dormitories at nine-forty-five. A policeman—a deportee with a green band on his arm—watches, more or less, that his charges are orderly and non-smoking. But red glowings and subdued murmurs continue for long.

Beneath this routine a ferment worked. Harding felt it as he listened in his bunk to all the actions and reactions of the Five Days, told again in the plain speech of the people, vivid, Rabelaisian, tragic. Murmur after murmur, question after question, story after story:

"Yes, we were in Jacob's and the holy father was hoisted up in the flour crane, one of the Franciscans from Church Street, a cheerful man with a long beard. And he told us to keep our hearts up, and we seen him after in Richmond Barracks with another Franciscan, and begor, them was the only smiling faces we seen for the whole bloody week between gougers shivering in their britches afraid they'd be shot and the solemn phisogs of the military looking at us as if we were going to eat them. Anyway, they arranged the surrender and we marched out to see a bloody great crowd, old ones gawking and chistlers cheering and old fellows with such bellies on them that they couldn't have seen their boots for twenty years talking as if they'd fought and won the whole bloody insurrection themselves, bejaney!

But anyway, the crowd let a bloody great cheer and bawled out: 'Did yous win?' So, we bawled back: 'No, we're bet this time!' So then be Jasus! the old ones started leaking and spilling and weeping all over the bloody shop till one of the old fellows bawls out again: 'Never mind, boys, yous did damned well for the first start off! Sure, the Archbishop will get yous all off.' And then the old ones cheered like bloody hell and half our lads, them not in uniform, shook hands with the other half and sloped home before the bloody military were the wiser."

"Them fellows had no right to slope home! Should have taken their chance with the rest like the young lad in our company, wouldn't give his right age because he knew they'd release him and he thought we were all for the barrack square and a firing party. 'And if yous go, I'll go,' says he."

"Shut up! You Post Office fellows have got swelled heads. We were too bloody scrupulous, fought too fair and kept all the rules. Why the hell shouldn't the lads slope home without asking the permission of that lot? One man out is worth twenty behind prison bars, and——"

"I was in Boland's Mill. In a long room full of flour sacks, and, begod, we wiped their bloody eyes—spreading rumours and hoisting tricolours on the distillery we occupied, too, till they didn't know where they were! Or how many we were. And we had a hotter time than yous had, and the big guns shaking the foundations, and us banging away at Beggar's Bush Barracks, and sending out a handful of lads to hold up the troops at Mount Street Bridge, and only two of them lads ever returned, all the others dead in the flames when the Tommies charged at last and bombed what was left. God, I was sorry for them lads. They were great stuff!"

"Ah, you should have been in the South Dublin Union with Eamonn Ceannt and Cathal Brugha. The troops broke in and near took the place, only a lad we all thought the greatest bloody fool and softy in the whole Dublin Brigade turned the tide sitting on the top of the stairs, lighting fuses and counting one, two, three and dropping bombs as cool as you please, and the bullets plastering the ceiling over his head. But they drove us back from the barricade inside, the pivot of the whole defence. Then Cathal Brugha—oh, ginger for pluck is no joke in his case! —stood behind it, an automatic in each hand, and between him and the lad on the top of the stairs the attack failed. We rushed back, and there was Cathal Brugha in a pool of blood, and he asked us to sing, 'God Save Ireland' before he died. And they took him away to hospital with seventeen bullets in him, and

41

in spite of all he's on the mend, although the military didn't bother to arrest him, he was that bad."

"Don't be talking! Galway was the place. Better than the pictures. Sean Condron's brother sitting under a tree and fellows galloping up and saluting him and dashing away with messages. Marching for days we were. And we took a barracks and a cruiser shelled the woods from the bay and I near blew the head off a bloody bobwee, so I did, only you couldn't see his backside for dust the first report. A wise peeler that!"

"We all know you are a great shot! You and your bobwee! O Mayo, God help us! Cromwell left the scum of Ireland there. Wild lads like you have us as we are. We done nothing, but here we are and no one to mind the farm at home."

"Ah, they can keep me here for ever if they feed me well. Gob, these gougers from Dublin calling themselves Generals and Commandants and Adjutants and Captains and drilling there in the compound and talking about more trouble!"

"Cranks and soreheads they call them, and small wonder!"

"Another rebellion! And I suppose that fellow, Mick Collins, who's always blowing out of him and shoving himself forward will be the leader. Christ, you'd think there was nowhere else but Cork and Dublin in the whole world. A lot of bastards who couldn't earn five bob a year!"

"You from the bog there! Shut up and let a man sleep!"

That fellow, Mick Collins! His name crept more and more into the whispered chronicle beneath the pilot light. And now to Harding the fantastic transformation of the man's shadow in O'Connell Street seemed less fanciful than before.

.   .   .   .   .   .

The camp dwindled by a hundred releases a day. The huts and the distillery grew barer and barer. One morning the little Welsh sergeant read out the names of Macken, Harding and Dick Blake. Twenty-four hours later they were back in Dublin.

CHAPTER V

HUGE presses singing, bells clanging, an inexorable clock ticking over his head, stooped at the sub-editorial desk—that was life for David Harding in the second six months after his return, life in the whirl, tumult and ordered litter of the *Emancipator*. The past, lulled by the singing machines, had grown dim in his

42

mind, but the day of his reunion with his old colleagues was a bright and pleasing memory. Michael Kerrigan, most senior of all *Emancipator* reporters, watched College Green from the steps of the new *Emancipator* office. He blew placid smoke-clouds from a stumpy briar, pig-blue eyes at rest, a bitter wisdom in his ponderous words:

"So you're back from the sword to the pen, are you? And they've made you a sub-editor, have they? Yerrah, is that a punishment or a decoration? What do you fellows want now? A new rebellion or a new party?"

Papa Shanahan came down the steps, sad and wrathful, although by nature most mellow of all *Emancipator* senior reporters. He nodded to Harding, asked for a match, lit his pipe and erupted. Fists clenched and eyes bulging, he called the heavens and earth to witness that within there was a lardy-faced, diminutive, bungling little Dungannon Know-all mis-called a General Manager, too busy making eyes at the ladies and sending the bloody paper to rack and ruin to mind his own business properly, too small to hit, all rump and pockets, begod, and the fellow, a thing unheard of in the history of any newspaper of standing, was demanding hotel bills for country trips before he'd shell out expenses, and, worse than that again, the Chief Reporter, or the News Editor, as he called himself since the new management raised his bloody screw, had passed on an editorial edict that a letter must be taken down in short-hand from a representative of the farming interests, a Mr. bloody Bill Gallagher, brains to the heels, Papa Shanahan didn't think, too lazy to take a pen in his paw——

"Yerrah," interrupted Michael Kerrigan stolidly. "Get a blank hotel bill, can't you? Is the General Manager a handwriting expert? Gob, he won't save money by asking for bills if the reporters of Ireland are the men I take them to be! As for poor Bill Gallagher, they have to humour the poor slob. He's a pull with advertisers, and he's dictated letters to the *Emancipator* for the past fifteen years. Sometimes he buys a copy. Perhaps, if your manners please him, he might stand you a drink."

"Let him keep his drinks," said Papa Shanahan with dignity, "for the porter sharks on his visiting list. I thought the new broom and the new management were at work. When we were the Party organ we were bothered by the fellows who never bought the paper, but wrote in and called in if we gave less than two columns to their speeches. Would the new thousand-a-year ornaments you meet mooning round the passages nowadays, washed-out descendants of Judas Iscariot, with bleached beards and haw-haw accents and watery eyes, take down Mr. Gallagher's pithy pars? Devil a sweet fear!"

"New broom!" snorted Michael Kerrigan. "What have we? Reporters without an outline of shorthand and contempt for the art! And sub-editors milking away in *saecula saeculorum!*"

Papa Shanahan winked at Harding, and then glanced anxiously at a passing *Liberator* van. He stroked his generous stomach and asked breathlessly:

"Did you see Bolger anywhere, Michael? He promised me a black of the Vigilance Committee?"

"No! I did not. Blacks! I never asked and gave one of those carbon copies in my life. I stand on me own two feet and me knowledge of Pitman's shorthand and no thanks to the fellows from the *Liberator* or any other paper on the face of the earth."

Papa Shanahan's eyes twinkled. His good humour returned. He tapped his forehead and turned to Kerrigan:

"Where's my memory? I've great news for you, and only you mentioned the subs and their game of milking the copy we write and telegraphing it to the ends of the earth so that it can be printed in every other paper but their own, I should have clean forgot to tell you that Thomas Bloody O'Kane, Prince of Milkers, was on retreat with the Jesuits last week and agrees with our point of view. He means it too. He's long-lived, for here he comes himself!"

Michael Kerrigan shot a neutral glance behind him. Thomas O'Kane—a dark, wiry, chalk-faced sub-editor, with bristle-specked jowl—was gliding down the stairs with feline motion, a bitter vacant smile, two full lips curling derisively, two sombre eyes swinging like pendulums behind thick glasses. Papa Shanahan shook with silent mirth as O'Kane paced round Michael Kerrigan, lean hands darted upwards, a voice purred, fingers dipped conciliatingly downwards into an elegant waistcoat pocket.

"I was talking to Shanahan, Michael Kerrigan, this morning," said O'Kane, smiling darkly. "And what I said to him I repeat to you. For ten years, as you have often pointed out, your copy has lain on the desk before me. And for more than ten years I have written my messages in my spare time as sub-editor, taken out my little book of telegraphic passes supplied to me by the papers for which I am correspondent——"

"The *Timbuctoo Gazette* and others," said Papa Shanahan eagerly. "Go on, O'Kane. Tell him what you told me!"

44

"What I said to Shanahan I repeat. I'll pay you full value for everything I have used since I first trimmed your invaluable copy."

Dulcet were the tones of Thomas O'Kane, and humbly stood he before the man he had wronged. Michael Kerrigan danced a few heavy steps and shouted:

"Ho! ho! The labourer is worthy of his hire. I'm glad the Jesuits rubbed the rust off your remembrance of the penny catechism. But better late than never!"

O'Kane's face went red, green, white and yellow, his voice lilted to a shriek, lightning flashed from the sombre pendulums, fingers dipping were now claws menacing aloft. There was a metallic ring at Michael Kerrigan's feet. Two farthings rolled and lay still.

"And there's liberal recompense!" screamed O'Kane. "And in addition I'll pay you a double bonus when any reporter on the *Emancipator* does start work." A whirl of arms and striding legs vanishing, and O'Kane's bitter vacant smile more bitter and vacant than before as it receded and was gone.

"Yerrah," said Michael, pocketing the two farthings. "So he admits the principles of the thing, and he'll be sick of the sight of these two farthings long before he remembers what the Jesuits told him as he sizzles on his bed of fire below for the wrong he has done the defenceless reporters of Ireland this twenty years, the old cod, digging in his garden during Easter week, instead of taking his chance with the lads, and blowing out of him now as bad as ever with his knife in the Party, trusted and pledge-bound and wrapped in the mantle Parnell wove around them."

Papa Shanahan suggested an Adjournment Across the Road. The Road led to Thomas O'Dea's "Diamond Bar" behind the Custom House. The proprietor, Thomas O'Dea of the grey whiskers, bright eyes and high colour. Papa Shanahan waved his glass with a lordly gesture, and told for the ten thousandth time the pleasant tale of the Pedantic Judge and the Rough-Spoken Witness and several others from the Liffeyside Decameron. Michael Kerrigan's memory stirred, and an encyclopaedia of information about sub-editors, with many cross-references and headings *in re* and *in extenso* and *inter pocula* and *in vino veritas* Thomas O'Kane, drummed in Harding's ears.

Suddenly Papa Shanahan sent up a great shout of welcome and Thomas P. Bolger of the *Liberator* was beside them, Thomas P. Bolger of the straight nose, foxy look and Christian name for all comers. He flourished a note and cried:

45

"The Press is damned droughty. Give it a name, boys!"

He clapped Papa Shanahan on the back, and drew a bulky wad from a bulging pocket:

"The black I promised you, Shanahan. I wouldn't miss that Vigilance Committee for a mint of money. There they sat spouting, about bad books and the sins of Dublin, and their Guardian Angels in a swoon beside them, and an old fellow with a grey beard and a greasy smile giving out all the spicy bits he heard in the music halls, and how they must watch out this month especially for the notorious Palpitating Popsey is booked for a turn at that hall on the quays. Then they appointed a deputation to visit the editors of the Dublin papers, and put bad thoughts in the heads of the poor men. And an old maid present got up and ballyragged them all, and then bejaney they set her over a committee to see the young folk of the city carry on their courting after a missioner's heart, under the eye of their das and mas and home by ten. Gob, there was a young fellow there from the *Irish Times*, and he blushed scarlet the things he heard. . . . But the poor ejots don't know what sin is. Now. . . !"

And Thomas P. Bolger unfolded his own amorous career from cradle to late middle-age, a lurid chronicle, most gravely told, of conquests in the most humble and exalted homes throughout the thirty-two counties of Ireland, while in several nonchalant asides he hinted that many Dubliners of resounding piety and renown were as brisk and persistent as himself in such matters —staunch and faithful members of the Order of St. Joseph, two heads on one pillow and never the same pillow twice.

Michael Kerrigan looked up and spat vigorously past Thomas P. Bolger's right ear. He moved his forehead back, shifted his ears and laughed with a weighty malice.

"I wonder the wife ever lets you out," he said with deliberation. "But sure you're harmless enough. Now shut up, for Jasus' sake. Yerrah, you fellows!"

As they went out, two men brushed past them, went through the bar, and with a nod to Thomas O'Dea ascended stairs, leading to an upper room. Harding recognised them: it was Michael Collins, with the dour and silent Tiger Doyle close on his heels. And when he reached the street he saw Dan Hogan watching in the shadows.

.   .   .   .   .   .

The sight of Michael Collins and the G-man reminded him of the flight of time. And the conflict in his own mind. Barely

46

six months had passed since Michael Collins had returned from Frongoch with the remaining deportees, and the Dublin crowds had cheered him and his comrades marching in their banned uniform in military formation in broad daylight, while the Castle, with centuries of experience to guide it, meekly looked on at the defiance of its proclamations, and sent Dan Hogan with a lorry load of soldiers to swoop a week later on a carefully prepared round of the seditious at midnight. . . . So tonight Dan Hogan was tracking Michael Collins, and watching. . . . Some day he would swoop. . . . Not tonight, that was not Dan's way. . . . For years he had tracked the leaders of Sinn Fein and haunted the meeting-places of the revolutionaries, his brain photographing their faces and each new face that appeared in the lecture halls, on the parades of the Volunteers, and lastly in the barrack squares and prisons. But to watch the new faces was a task beyond him now. . . . Outside the barrack doors the young men were drilling and swooping into mansions and farmhouses and coastguard stations in search of arms when the shades fell.

It was a twelvemonths since the Insurrection. On his return he had interviewed the Editor of the *Emancipator*, who had told him that although the flames of Easter Week had destroyed the old office, and the men of Easter Week had used the type to make bullets and bombs, the *Emancipator* would rise again under a new management, with a new policy and a new staff, in six months. So Harding wrote a letter to the editor and the editor wrote a letter to Harding appointing him a sub-editor, and Harding rode off to wait until the builders had finished. This change in Harding's status won only a qualified approval from Papa Shanahan, but to all his protests and questions, Harding answered:

"I want to think."

For to Harding Easter Week had brought a crisis. He was staring, staring, staring at a mental blank wall. A wall of doubt and disillusion, the deep foundations of which disappeared beneath the debris of the Five Days when Tom Hughes had mounted guard at the open windows and lamented his poems against war in Jim Larkin's *Worker*. Tom Hughes's chance remark always seemed the last stone laid upon a wall; the first stone had been laid long before, and the wall had mounted even as the Great War broke, and Harding drilled beside his Volunteer comrades. Sometimes as the drill terms rang out in the little mill or as Bernard Milroy burst into a fierce oration, he became conscious of the conflict in his mind, the appeal of the works of Tolstoy or the moving lines of a Quaker dreamer of the seventeenth century:

"There is a spirit which I feel which delights to do no evil, nor to revenge any wrong, but delights to endure all things in hope to enjoy its own in the end. Its hope is to outlive all wrath and contention, and to weary out exaltation and cruelty or whatever is of a nature contrary to itself. It sees to the end of all temptations. As it bears no evil in itself it conceives none in thoughts to any other. If it be betrayed it bears it, it bears it, for its ground and spring is the mercies and forgiveness of God. Its crown is meekness, its life is everlasting love unfeigned; and it takes its kingdom with entreaty and not with contention, and keeps it by lowliness of mind."

A deeper and as eloquent appeal as that had stirred him in the Great Strike of Nineteen Thirteen, when the social fabric had shaken and quivered for half a year, and some thirty thousand workers had tightened their belts and said they would stand by Jim Larkin's Union in spite of all the powers of the employers leagued against them to enforce the ban. He had listened to the Labour evangelists, and had been led to the literature of anti-militarism and Socialism, and met in lecture rooms the missionaries of the Labour International spreading their pamphlets and clashing with the deep-rooted Nationalism of Ireland, in all the accents of Europe and America.

And on the eve of Nineteen Sixteen itself, while one side of his brain flamed to enthusiasm at the tricolour soon to wave among the many standards of the Great War, another side ached with the nightmare of human agony on the battlefields. And for a time his riddle was answered. What did it matter? Any blow against that infamy, no matter what and by whom, was good enough for him, and to harden his mood came the city employers "releasing" their workers to the trenches in thousands, the blaring bands, the recruiting posters, the sharp curve of the constitutional politicians. . . .

But from the Easter ashes rose the old riddle once more. To shoot or not to shoot? The question obsessed him. Guns, guns, guns, words, words. . . . The new Invisible Army and the new legends of the new militarists, a minority changed overnight into a majority with all the vices and tricks of the old Party it was now sweeping aside. . . . A dullness, a nausea, a longing for any other sheen than the sheen of arms, an inward war between head and heart. . . . Between himself and his books and between himself and the glorious Irish country-side through which he rode, trying to forget, rose the relentless questions:

"Will you press the trigger? What have you in common with this new movement but a danger shared with a handful?" And he knew he would not press the trigger although the faces of Clarke and MacDermott and Milroy loomed over all his waking hours, over all the aching thought circles of his brain. Well, then, do what? He dissected the deadness of his spirit, the frayed nerves, the ebb and flow of thought enthusiasm and scepticism. The more it changed, the more it was the same, even with the Easter memories and the danger of his comrades tugging at his heartstrings like some old tragic love memory. All politicians were the same in the hour of victory . . . they shed what had made them great before . . . these discredited and betrayed autocrats in the rags of Parnell's mantle that the youth of Ireland and British politicians together were casting aside, old melancholy babbling shades, shadows of what once was great . . . these new ones would be the same, these new ones gambling with guns and keeping all compliments for the anniversaries of their enemies' funerals. . . . Claiming agreement not on ninety-nine points, but on a hundred. . . . Droning their propaganda, lie for lie, slogan for slogan, fable for fable, slander for slander. . . . Right perhaps. . . . What had Macken said when he had told him of these views: "If we sit down and think we should all say the same, and that would be fatal." Words, words, words, words, guns, guns, guns, guns. . . . Cowardice? No, you could clear out if you wanted to!

And who would clear out? Even as he bicycled about the countryside, with the wheels singing beneath him, he knew that Michael Collins and his comrades were running the King of Thessaly's son very close in the race.

Everywhere was the sign of coming change. As he went down the western coast from Galway two meetings lingered in his mind. In Galway he had met Terence O'Donovan, still in khaki and on leave. Half an hour before it had seemed to him that Dublin's ferment was as nothing beside the message of the earth and the menace of the skies, the crops, the beasts and the long evenings. The childhood of the world lingered in Connacht's very speech and legends. There was Galway, with its dark and pronounced people, crumbling mansions of former merchants in the days of a vanished commercial glory, the quaint architecture, the shady walks by the Corrib. And then he had met Terence O'Donovan, gloomy, pensive, a gonfalon, a war banner ever, in his eyes. And Terence sketched for Harding the vast and bloody monotony of the Western front, the shell-holes, the lice, the smell and the eternal orchestra of the guns, a wilderness of shell-holes yawning up villages, a terror the Irish country-side had never known, not even in the days when Elizabethan armies had left Munster a desert and when Cromwell had come with psalms and slaughter, not now in rich and fertile quiet. . . . And how he had heard Michael Collins haranguing the Invisible Army in a western town, and wondered whether the few hundred men with faces alight and their pathetic antiquated weapons knew what war was, and the strength in millions of war-hardened veterans, who would tramp homewards some day when the constant drip of Allied blood had worn away the solid German stone. . . . But the personality of Michael Collins held O'Donovan. There were hundreds of Michael Collinses in the wilderness of shell-holes, listening to the eternal orchestra. . . .

Easter Week held Terence O'Donovan too, and he made Harding tell him again and again the things he had seen and heard. In Terence O'Donovan ancestral instincts wrestled with present loyalties. He sighed and said half to himself: "When this war ends, the wars will not end for me. Only for this Army oath, even now——" And his eyes seemed to search the horizon for something he would never find, and a pensive greyness which overcast his haggard and war-worn features was lighted by a sudden flash of enthusiasm, the iron self-reliance which nerved him in an eternal quest in his wilderness amidst the orchestra of guns, the horror, the stench, the dead, fighting for a cause in which he no longer believed. . . . And in his quest, Terence was staring at a mental blank wall too—a tragic granite man, gentle and with a spell in his thoughtful, courteous words.

Among Iar-Chonnacht's hills and the Joyce country, and the Twelve Pins dominating all, Harding came upon a camp in a remote and sheltered place. A figure which had been a shade since Easter Eve came to life, a name whispered in the Post Office, a name Sergeant Jolly had mentioned in the prison: Dermott Considine, the poet, a thin, spare, intense young man of thirty-two with prominent, haunted grey eyes. The dark-visaged Tiger Doyle was there too. And the Tiger told Harding the Easter failure over which Considine had brooded since his release:

"It was not his fault. He was on the spot waiting for the arms to be run in. But no arms arrived. Different orders came. He walked round half-mad with grief, though where was he to blame when there were divisions in Dublin and he had no arms for his men, and one fellow saying he would go this way and

50

another lad saying he would go that, and the military with tremendous great guns trained on the Volunteer hall before you could wink?"

Considine and the Tiger drilled some thirty men in the evenings. In small cottages Harding saw the portraits of the Easter Week leaders, and once, when he spoke in a small Sinn Fein club, he was startled when a name he mentioned and a phrase he quoted sent echoes wrathful and stormy ringing through the room: the name of Tom Clarke and a phrase of Pearse. And so well did he know the drill halls of Dublin that he saw, before the echoes died away, Michael Collins dividing this cheering crowd into a battalion, appointing its leaders with a glance of his keen grey-blue eyes and a curt word.

He told Considine of the Five Days and MacDermott and O'Rahilly's death and Michael Collins and his own restless mood. But Considine smiled and said that was but youth, and then with glowing eyes, the spectre of his Easter failure goading him on, he said that the Republic would not die, and that the Republic was a thing all the power of Terence O'Donovan's comrades returning would never kill. The Invisible Army would win all that the men who had died at Easter had demanded with their blood. And for his own part he would never take nineteen and sixpence when he could get a pound, though wise men and leaders of the people had told him in confidence that they feared they would only get ten and sixpence in the end. . . . But what use was this talk of loss and gain? He quoted Whitman's words: "Death and defeat are great."

"Easy for you to talk!" added the Tiger Doyle, with a bitter smile, in answer to a question. "You had your whack, David Harding, but some of us will have to go on fighting till we drop. I will!"

And in his eyes Harding read anger and remorse, and he remembered the words of Michael Collins: "Young Doyle was caught . . . under a lamp-post beside the cart and planks . . . in the windows across the way, the Tiger Doyle himself looking down into the street, with a face as white as a fish's belly on his dead brother below." And yet the Tiger had walked into the Rising in the end. What circles in the brain, what heart-searchings, what agonies of the spirit those Five Days had caused! And in a flash he knew that the Irish Revolution would sweep on even to those quiet hills.

Away back at last on whirring wheels to Dublin, through a flat and uneventful landscape, but with the dark scowl of the

Tiger Doyle and the dark sayings of Dermott Considine much in his thoughts.

   •   •   •   •   •   •

Back to huge singing presses and the inexorable clock and Michael Kerrigan and Papa Shanahan. Back to his little room in Drumcondra. Back to the Queen of Cities, with her face in its hundred moods; her great noble churches and the lamps, pious red and blue, which flashed out on many a mean street, beacons of other-worldly beauty in the homes of the poor; the shuttered windows behind which Michael Collins hid his young men to drill and toil in their bomb factories; tenements with emetic stench and half the city's families doomed for life to their two rooms there; the sea of heads worshipping in the crowded churches, the army of feet hammering the pavements after the Sunday Masses; the masts and quays of dockland; the isolated mansions of Rathmines and Rathgar's respectable villas; sea-gulls swooping and skimming sea and sands from Merrion to Killiney; the winding paths and gleaming lighthouse and great waters beyond Howth Hill; all Dublin's murmurs, harsh and musical; all Dublin's joy of life and age-wise melancholy; flashes of divinity and golden hope breaking through murk-laden and leaden airs, high, high above the whole conglomeration of dwellings, monuments, club rooms, dram shops and human warrens seawards out to the hills, a jest on a hundred thousand lips whatever sorrows vex memories or bones.

And the *Emancipator* was a very sentinel tower to Dublin, albeit the most prosaic happenings or the most romantic or the most soul-searing had to be fitted beneath a certain number of letters when not pigeon-holed or flung into the waste-paper baskets or recorded only in brief phrases by Michael Kerrigan and Papa Shanahan in the Reporters' Room or dismissed to obscurity with a shake of the editor's head. Colder than the warm and living truth in any case when reshaped on the desks and locked in the printers' formes and thrown to the clicking linotypes and the great presses beneath the white globes, warm living truth drowned in the shriek of the bold black type of those posters on the *Emancipator's* doors, those perpetually shrieking riddles Thomas O'Kane's cunning composed to set all Dublin's nerves jumping and draw Dublin's pennies into the *Emancipator's* till.

And in this sentinel tower Harding settled down with this pageant before him of a capital, and Michael Collins rising daily into deeper type to the song of the presses, pursued and hunted in vain, a new and terrible world on his broad shoulders. . . .

The *Emancipator's* presses sang an unanswered question: whither, whither, whither? And David Harding, bewildered by it all, ignored his blank wall, and knew only that he must wait, steadfast, till the last notes of the song were finished.

CHAPTER VI

DICK BLAKE, on the other hand, found that Michael Collins had brought a new excitement into his life. He worked out his days on the docks and returned in the evenings to his little daughter, May, in the rooms over a shop on the quays the windows of which commanded a view of the Custom House and the shipping gliding down the Liffey. It was really on three evenings a week he lived now in the little mill among the hills with his thirty comrades. But Dick's life was a tenser and more dangerous life than before. Dick Blake could hit a halfpenny at God alone knew how many yards, and Michael Collins knew it. And Dick Blake had a mask of a face and the patience of Job, and Michael Collins knew it. Thus it came that Sean Condron and Dick Blake held many mysterious conferences with a view to plans maturing in Michael Collins's brain even while raids, arrests and street searches nibbled at the officers and arsenals of the I.R.A. and the wise folk of Ireland laughed and said that soon those wild lads would be out of harm's way, and to strengthen them in their wisdom the London newspapers ran streamers across their pages now and then: THIS IS THE END OF SINN FEIN. And sometimes the *Liberator* and the *Emancipator* read the wild young men a sermon, but in general had something more homely to fill their columns with.

Dick Blake's little daughter, May, was a chip of the old block. She was unconcerned when bulky packages disappeared under the flooring of the front room, to be collected by young men in trench coats and slouch hats. Nor was she surprised when young men sometimes dropped in and slept in the front room without warning. She knew that the bulky packages were arms and ammunition and the young men were "on the run," and that meant very badly wanted by the Castle. They remained in the front room until a seafaring man called and took them aboard beyond Dan Hogan's scrutiny or grasp. May herself marched in the great processions in a green uniform and learned about bandages and wounds and the makes of arms in a city

53

drill hall, and venerated Madame Markievicz, whose only fault was to call Ireland "Ahland" and tell thick ejots at public meetings—who never meant to do a hand's turn for "Ahland," for bejaney a bobby had only to frown at them and you wouldn't see their backsides for dust—never to go out in such stirring times as these without "a little friend like this," flourishing a revolver, and all the gougers cheering fit to burst their throats but never meaning to fire a shot in anger themselves. A bit mad Madame Markievicz was, but mad in the right way and good to the poor and full of spirit, though her hair had turned white in jail and the rotten *Emancipator* hinting that she had reneged her principles by taking out a licence for her pet dog, Angelface. Sean Condron and Arthur Macken and all the others coming and going in the front room were mad in the right way too. And there was little need to cheer and weep over plays like *Wolfe Tone* in the Queen's Theatre from the gallery, so intense was life at home now. . . . Though it had been great gas to boo the informer and clap at Napoleon grinding his teeth at the white cliffs of England but going to Egypt after all the greatest mistake of his career through not listening to Wolfe Tone in his white britches waving his sword and telling the French he didn't give a fig for any other country but his own, and the "gods" howling like demons, and you had to sit tight in your seat and not look round or you might get a sucked-out orange or the core of an apple in the kisser, and spits—saving your presence—flying each side of your ears anyway from ignorant old fellows showing what they were and old ones ready to give you a clump of an umbrella if you laughed at the heroine in distress.

●　　　●　　　●　　　●　　　●　　　●

Sometimes a burst of laughter came from the corner of the upstairs room over Thomas O'Dea's, where Michael Collins and a party of young men were gathered. The songs stopped and Mick was called upon. He sat in his corner, looking in front of him lost in thought. He rose abruptly with his hands in his pockets, scanned the ceiling and the floor and recited "Kelly and Burke and Shea," shaking his head defiantly, and chanted until with the closing lines a passion and an assurance came into his voice:

> *"Oh, the fighting races don't die out,*
> *If they seldom die in bed,*
> *For love is first in their hearts, no doubt."*
> *Said Burke; then Kelly said:*

"When Michael, the Irish Archangel, stands,
The angel with the sword,
And the battle dead from a hundred lands
Are ranged in one big horde,
Our line that for Gabriel's trumpet waits,
Will stretch three deep that day,
From Jehosaphat to the Golden Gates—
Kelly and Burke and Shea."
"Well, here's thank God for the race and the sod!"
Said Kelly and Burke and Shea.

Whereupon Michael Collins nodded to the company and sat down modestly before the echoes of his tense Cork accent had died away.

Thomas O'Dea came in, and thereafter Mick's laughter chorused six of Thomas's favourite stories of the quaint characters who drifted in and out of his Family Grocery, and the long procession of crooks, twisters, humbugs and rogues he had known, and Mick's protests drowned Thomas O'Dea's appeals to the young men to give Dominion Home Rule a chance.

"Dry up, you old twister! Dominion Home Rule is all bloody bunk! We want a Republic!"

"All right, Mick," said Thomas O'Dea. "As you will, but consider at least——"

"Constitutional balderdash!" shouted Michael Collins, and turned the company back to songs, Thomas O'Dea's stories, reminiscences and toasts. A boon companion and born leader rolled into one, with a good Gascon spicing.

Sean Condron and Arthur Macken came in and spoke to him in low tones: Dan Hogan was below.

"Never mind the louser!" roared Michael Collins. "There is too much bloody G-manitis in this bloody city for my taste. Half the bloody jails are filled by bloody fellows sprinting across the road when they see a policeman."

Macken shrugged his shoulders and completed his message: the Tiger was over in Agnes MacGowan's with a message from Considine. Mick recovered his good humour. He rose with a genial smile and twinkling eyes: "The Tiger among the highbrows. Let's go round and put him out of pain."

Mick clattered down the stairs and strode into the street. He wheeled his bicycle past Dan Hogan, the G-man, who stepped towards him with greedy eyes and a malicious smile. Mick threw his leg over the cross-bar and scowled at the detective. His hand went to his hip pocket and a wave of hatred into his

55

grey-blue eyes—a wave of menace and memory almost physical.
The detective went white and stepped back. Michael Collins
looked him in the face for a minute.

"Behave yourself, Dan Hogan," he said. "You have had a
very full warning."

Michael Collins rode away. Hogan stood looking after him.
A burly policeman came up and joined him. Hogan muttered:

"Behave myself! What corner boy of the lot of them would
have the guts to hurt me in spite of all their threatening letters?
That bloody Cork ejot is behind all the devilment with his name
on all the documents we captured of late—Michael Collins or
M.C. or Mick, Adjutant-General or Commander-in-Chief or
Head Cook and Bottle Washer, I.R.A. I'll put a stop to his
gallop before the night is out. A nice state of affairs! You
can't show your nose these times without these fellows making
a scene. Can't take their medicine like sensible men. Walking
through jail walls they are and breaking the hearts of every jail
governor in Ireland. Jug a few of them, shoot a few more, and
let half a dozen of them starve themselves into Hell on the next
hunger strike! Isn't one bloody rebellion enough for them? No
sympathy for a plain decent man doing his plain decent duty."

"Gob, you're a temerarious man, Dan Hogan," said the burly
policeman. Without further words, Hogan vanished into the
network of lanes which brought him to the Central Police Station.
A group of youths in waterproofs and soft hats lounged near
Trinity College railings opposite. Dick Blake was in their midst.
Macken and Condron spoke to the group when they emerged
from the laneway some moments after Hogan. The men scattered
casually into Grafton Street. Dick Blake remained at the railings chatting to Tom Hughes, who waited, one foot on the pedal
of his bicycle. A military lorry dashed up to the police station.
Hogan rushed out and jumped into it, his coal-black eyes glowing. Tom Hughes pedalled at full speed out of sight as the lorry
lumbered slowly round Trinity College, Hogan chatting excitedly
to the officer in charge, the Tommies grinning amiably at the
pedestrians—bayonets jutting above trench helmets.

"This time I'll catch the bastard," said Hogan, "and he'll
laugh the other side of his face."

•   •   •   •   •   •   •

Macken and Condron rang the bell of Mrs. MacGowan's
flat, and looked up at the tall house in Upper Mount Street
with its high windows. Light, noise and laughter from the top
storey told them that Agnes MacGowan was holding one of her

famous tea-parties. A young man in soft hat and trench coat opened the door. Tom Hughes was behind him, still grasping his bicycle. The young man shrugged his shoulders sceptically as Hughes dashed into the street again.

In the animated room above, Michael Collins sat silently beside the Tiger Doyle, mute and glowering in a corner. Mick's eyes were bent on a sheaf of documents, firmly clutched. Ladies in Gaelic robes, vivacious young men in leggings, riding britches, smoking Kapp and Peterson pipes and revolvers bulging in their hip pockets and Patrick Edward MacGowan occupied three sofas. Patrick Edward MacGowan, eloquent in the Law Courts on occasion, invariably smoked an enormous pipe in company, a half-sad, half-amused look alert in his sombre eyes.

Agnes MacGowan stood in the centre of the room, a curious blend of force and sweetness in the eagerness and torrent of her words, a clash of youth and age in the fairness of her features, laughing her bitter-honey laugh, moods very sudden and varied in the changing mirror of her merry blue eyes.

In the middle of the room, on a cushion, a girl of sixteen was shouting at a shock-haired youth:

"None of your excuses! Why weren't you out with your company? When the flag went up, why did you leave them in the lurch? My brother was shot, my brother was shot, my brother was shot, and I'll take none of your excuses!"

Two bald professors argued with a priest at the other end of the room. Great men in circles discussed each other's books and waved beards and incense at each other and scanned each other's faces closely and suspiciously, self-conscious mortals in perpetual limelight annoyed by the thunder of neighbouring Oracles, Minor Poets, Casual Playwrights and Free Lance Essayists. The young men on the sofas glanced towards them from time to time, lips curling behind fuming pipes. The men of war dismissed the Literati with a whiff of nicotine. The young girl droned her litany, never leaving the protesting youth alone, the youth who never thought to retort that brothers were being shot all over the world, the fashion then. Agnes rattled malicious question after question as she moved through the smoke-clouds over the chatting groups. Through the open window came the faint hum of a motor engine. "My brother was shot, my brother was shot, my brother was shot"—the proud and reproaching litany sounded above every other egomaniacal chorus in the room.

"Pity it wasn't you, you snivelling bitch!" snarled the Tiger Doyle, rising in a sudden fury, his dark eyes on fire. He went out and slammed the door violently behind him. A silence fell on the room, shocked by the passion and rage in the Tiger's cry. Louder through the open window hummed the approaching engines of a heavy lorry.

"The poor Tiger!" lisped Agnes sweetly. "*His* brother was shot. He funked, you know."

"The Tiger was in hotter places during Easter Week than you were, Agnes," said Michael Collins sharply. Agnes winced, ignored the remark, and serenely tore Fifty Martial Reputations to shreds. Mick turned discreetly back to his papers, muttering in irritation to himself. Great Men waved beards again, the young men laughed loudly, the talk flowed on, and beneath the ebb and flow the Great Tide sweeping through Ireland, sweeping human wills before it. . . .

A whistle sounded downstairs, a lorry's engine howled under the window, a hammering on the door reverberated up four flights. . . . Michael Collins rose quietly and vanished. . . . Noise of a window opening, a scrunching sound, a rattle of slates falling, a rush of feet on the stairs. . . . Dan Hogan towered over the khakied raiders in the doorway.

"Mr. Collins has just left," said Agnes sweetly. "He said he met you this afternoon."

Hogan pursed his mouth and the young men on the sofas eyed him like hawks and then laughed loudly. "Nothing worth taking among these cods and corner boys," he said with a ponderous contempt. "Come on." The khaki forms disappeared. Great Men waved their beards . . . the talk flowed on.

·　　　·　　　·　　　·　　　·　　　·

Michael Collins stirred from the coping stone against which he had lain hidden, clambered up the sloping slates, went down the stairs, and, looking neither right nor left, cycled away—his dark hair waving in the wind.

CHAPTER VII

THE presses sang the passing of the Great War and the coming of that new Ireland which Michael Collins and his Invisible Army ruled. Under Harding's headings the shadow of a Little War crept into larger, deeper and more challenging type. But it was not always the national tragedy that moved him or the national comedy, but the *Emancipator* itself, and the unknown world within the *Emancipator*. This world had its moments of fascination and tragedy as full and deep as that wider world which was recorded in its columns every day.

The *Emancipator* had a place of romance and antiquity in journalistic annals. In derisive allusion to one of Ireland's many names in Gaelic legend, a Dublin wit had once christened the paper the *Poor Old Woman*. The *Phoenix*, however, would have been a juster nickname, for the *Emancipator* renewed its youth once in every half-century. Its files covered many stirring pages of Irish history for thirty years before the Union and every varied phase henceforward. Members of the staff who had joined it in their boyhood and early youth had recollections which reached back to the rise and fall of Parnell.

"Begod," Michael Kerrigan was wont to declare in pessimistic moods, "no one loves the Poor Old Woman." But when Harding rejoined the staff, Michael's dark cloud had been lined with generous silver. In the first place, the British Government had showed in unmistakable ways that it did not love the *Emancipator*, and, in the second place, the paper had been reorganised with new capital, and the new management had given the paper a force and vitality which displeased its rivals and the Castle. Long speeches (though Michael criticised this) went into the waste-paper baskets and more news (and this delighted Michael, proudest and most relentless of newsgatherers) into the once solemn columns of the paper. Thomas O'Kane was told to go ahead with his posters, and dignity be damned, and he went ahead with such effect that not only the Dubliners bought the *Emancipator* in thousands, their curiosity fired daily, and their hearts missing a beat, but even Thomas P. Bolger three times a week bought a copy of the *Emancipator*, and then cursed Thomas O'Kane for fooling him into paying for what he already knew. These posters had another aspect, best told in the words of Papa Shanahan:

"I declare to high Heaven we'll hit a rock for every morning I look at the posters, not knowing what's coming next. Instead of 'Ireland Divided' for a partition scheme, or something dull and safe like that, it's 'O Protoplasmic Infamy!' or 'Hail, Thou Glorious Dawn!' And every day we tell off the Castle the way a daily newspaper never told off the Castle in the city of Dublin before. I have it straight from the horse's mouth, they don't like it. Abuse, calling them scoundrels within reason, they can stand, but the jeering has ruffled the Red Hats. Some night O'Kane will let rip in the vernacular, and we'll perish in the ruins."

"What matter?" cried Michael Kerrigan with scorn. "At this crisis of our country's fate, it behoves all men who guide the opinion of the public to make a firm stand and eschew the counsels of the lily-livered. We're right this time, begod, we are. The poor old *Emancipator* has always backed a losing horse, but never has the British Government been right in this country yet. Michael Kerrigan, loyal to the Party, but no dog-in-the-manger to efforts of those, who, by the suffrages of the electorate, for the moment guide and control the nation, Michael Kerrigan tells ye that. Aye, here I stand in the Bearna Baoghail, the Gap of Danger, begod. I love me country. I love every blade of grass. 'And how can man die better than by facing fearful odds for the ashes of his fathers and the temples of his gods?' " And he danced a stately measure on the floor of the Reporters' Room. And later swept with dignity to the telephone to proclaim: "My Lord Mayor of Dublin, this is the *Emancipator* ringing you up." Then away with himself and Papa Shanahan and their friendly competitor, Thomas P. Bolger, like knight errants into strange lands, knowing Harding's headlines and O'Kane's posters would herald all they found in their quests.

·   ·   ·   ·   ·   ·   ·

The *Emancipator* knew of tragedies within its walls, however, which no poster and barely a headline heralded. The short lines, "We regret to state that Mr. Thomas Mill, a very old member of our staff, died in a city hospital yesterday," followed by the names of many Dublin journalists who attended the funeral, remained unnoticed by many readers. Yet Harding read nothing in that morning's paper with keener interest. For often when he had gone down to the Reporters' Room he had noticed a fine old man with a small white spike of a beard and merry blue eyes scrawling in a microscopic hand on small pages.

Printers scowled when they read that microscopic hand, and Thomas Mill always admitted their grievance, and his merry eyes lighted up when he saw a clear flowing hand and a colleague who used copy paper lavishly: "That's right, my boy! Paper is cheap. Don't copy my bad habits." Michael Kerrigan sniffed with contempt at Thomas Mill, for Thomas Mill insisted that Pitman's shorthand might have its good points, but for his part he would remain loyal to the fine and ancient system invented by Mr. Gurney long before Michael Kerrigan had been thought of.

And when Michael grew eloquent in defence of Pitman, the best friend the poor reporter ever had, begob, a twinkle would creep into Thomas Mill's eyes and he would murmur:

"He was Sir Isaac before he died, and that's more than any reporter will ever be. No, plain Mr. Gurney for me."

And when Michael grew abusive, Thomas looked up and said:

"Tut, tut, my good man. You have few ideas and fewer words to express them."

When a reply followed, Thomas rose, laughing:

"Ah, I rejoice to have got beneath the fur of the animal."

Something about this old man attracted Harding, and he liked the austere and generally silent figure in the corner of the Reporters' Room who was then twenty years past his half-century. Sometimes Harding heard him break his silence. It was when the blue eyes lighted to a youthful fire and the noble old figure drew itself up, and a generation's memories became vocal in the hushed and reverent words, with their Northern tang, and Parnell ruled immense crowds again with haughty snaps of the fingers and enkindling phrases:

"Parnell, Parnell! I heard them silent, yes, heard them silent, no other word will fit, in their thousands round them, as he told them that he held Ireland's freedom in the hollow of his hand. . . . Ah, what a man he was, a man, a most potent man . . . and they threw him to the English wolves!"

In a score of newspaper offices had he clothed this name in flesh and blood, but in his seventieth year he worked on space in the *Emancipator*. One night his obituary notice and the details of his funeral flashed under Harding's eyes. Papa Shanahan explained in the "Diamond Bar" later:

"Poor old Mill has gone the way we all go if we live long enough. He went to a meeting he was marked for at the last moment and he had left his overcoat at home and got drenched to the skin and wrote up his account in the office dripping wet and stuck the bloody *Liberator* for three facts to the joy of the bloody Chief Reporter and went home and caught pneumonia and was taken to hospital where he raved and the only way the nurses could quieten him was to hand him paper and he wrote and wrote in his queer old fist and handed out each page to the nurse to take down to the printer. . . . God rest his soul."

· · · · · · ·

But not only in headings and reports and posters crept the shadow of Michael Collins and the Little War for Ireland, but into the placid home in Drumcondra of Mrs. Brownbill of the kindly face and mellow eyes. A long tradition of students had been a tradition with her, never more than three at a time for

61

eleven years, and she thought she had exhausted all surprises in the pranks and follies of men. Students had painted her walls with scraps and skeletons and the human viscera and darkened the windows and called up the spirits of the dead in the glow of Chinese lanterns, and hired pipers and harpers and wandered away to the South Circular Road, to be enticed into buying up the stock in trade of Jewish shops, and arrived home with parcels of Guinness, of which she relieved them until morning. For eleven years they had come and gone and blossomed into doctors and professors and travellers and famous men.

Into this quiet place came Sean Condron and Dick Blake on Saturday nights to visit Harding, and sometimes they slept there when Mick sent them the word that a lorry might call at midnight elsewhere. On Saturday nights they talked to a late hour, and in Sean Condron's accents sounded the new Ireland which had swept aside the softness and eloquence and romanticism of the old Ireland, living with its finger on the trigger and a hard glint in its eye. One night Dick Blake entered, very mysterious and very pleased with himself. A vaguely familiar figure came behind him. Harding looked up from a well-thumbed volume of Montaigne's *Essays*. It was Terence O'Donovan in strange civilian garb. But his talk soon ran on gun-running and new companies of the Invisible Army. The Great War was a thing of yesterday and the Peace Conference too, but Terence O'Donovan was with Michael Collins now, and through his speech glowed and burned the implacable spirit of revolution, a hard, electric, universal flame. And Harding heard the feet of history in the relentless and enthusiastic words of O'Donovan, the smile of Sean Condron and the shrug of Dick Blake's shoulders.

Terence O'Donovan reached across for the volume of Montaigne, and smiled.

"That is the right book to read," he said, "in days like our own. Lend it to me, Harding. It will be safe unless they capture me and my flying column in the South next week."

CHAPTER VIII

ARTHUR MACKEN hurried swiftly through Lower Baggot Street en route to the outlying Dublin suburb where Michael Collins awaited him. His thoughts hurried too, there was a glint in his keen eyes and a concentrated look on his lean pallid face. From time to time his hand felt the Webley revolver in the breast pocket of his greatcoat while he pedalled feverishly over tram sets and cobble-stones. Since his release from Frongoch a new philosophy had gripped Macken.

Events had swept him into a highly charged atmosphere where a cold-blooded minority leavened a seething and fiery mass. He was one of the new revolutionaries, with them, at least, if not wholly of them, insolent, hard-headed, calculating young men who believed in action, "on the run," perpetually in and out of jail, hunger-striking, and just now shooting. A handful which in two short years had swept their opponents from power while the writ of their Invisible Republic ran throughout the country. Grim things were done. He had done them himself, wondering at the blend of callousness and scrupulosity which invaded him by turns. How time had sped on! It seemed hardly yesterday since he had stood outside Frongoch and found himself back in Dublin while the Great War dragged along. The Great War vanished in one burst of Union Jacks in Dublin's more prosperous streets. . . . Then came the lingering and omni-present Little War. . . . And troops poured in for this Little War, spreading daily from the South.

Murder? What about the Boers and Spaniards? Hadn't they sniped and struck and run, aye, and worse? Anyway, Michael Collins didn't call it murder, though his very name made many a Red Hat scarlet with rage and pallid with fear. . . . "Head of the whole murder gang." . . . Oh, here was the house.

Macken passed through an iron gate and entered one of the temporary headquarters of Michael Collins; he had twenty others spread over Dublin, but Dan Hogan had never found one yet. And if Dan knew why! His most confidential reports copied before the ink was dry on them, his sources of informa-tion known, used and shadowed. . . .

There was a small crowd within. The Tiger Doyle was there, Sean Condron and Tom Hughes, a young woman and her little daughter. Michael Collins was playing with the child, who had just tearfully appealed to him against the teasing of Tom Hughes and Sean Condron. Michael Collins shook his fist in mock indignation at the tormentors, to the child's relief and delight. She waved her fair curls and prattled gaily, offering him her doll in gratitude, which he refused with solemnity and again shook his fist at Sean Condron disparaging the doll's appear-ance. . . . Friends of his people, he said in an aside to Macken, adding he must hurry back to his work. The party retired, the child waving many kisses to Mick. He smiled, winked at Macken and drew a mass of documents towards him.

Five minutes passed. A man entered apologetically. Mick brandished his watch at him:

"Ten minutes late, you louser! Go away and come back in six hours and ten minutes. Don't think because you are a Commandant you can walk over me and time. Get out, and quick!" Grinning pathetically, the Commandant withdrew. Mick spluttered and muttered to himself.

Macken's eyes ran round the room. It was trim and business-like, martial and overcrowded. Presses stuffed with documents, several tables laden with newspaper files, copies of *The Times* and *Manchester Guardian* scattered around. And small stacks of revolvers, trench-knives, ammunition; beneath boxes of explosives and a rope ladder. Within the walls, Mick's invariable secret cupboards which had baffled many a raid when he vacated one hiding-place, and Dan Hogan and a midnight lorry had blundered into an empty nest.

On the desk in front of him, neat heaps of reports and bundles of papers were ranged round the typewriter—these and a glance at the maps on the walls, and Mick knew every man hostile, friendly or useful to him and the theatres and fortunes of the Little War. Sometimes Mick worked twelve, fifteen, even eighteen hours a day, going on till he dropped. A lion for work.

Barely two or three years ago this young man was unknown. Unknown to the readers of his escapes. Unknown to those who were thrilled by a sudden legend sweeping from the Dublin gossips and the British Secret Service to fill the columns of the world's press. But the London-Irish had known the son of the Clonakilty farmer listening to the Hyde Park orators with intent ear and twinkling eye, shocking staid enthusiasts among the exiles with his whirlwind manner and expletives, an alert and dashing figure on the hurling or football field, orating in the political clubs or hanging over the galleries of the London theatres. Then in the restless days after the Insurrection he had emerged. Why none knew. A curious power emanated from him, and by some inborn genius he had gone onward, unaided, to the leadership of the Invisible Army. Dan Hogan had Michael Collins well recorded in his memory and saw that in that one personality the inspiration of all the calculated defiance which broke down prison discipline, hunger-struck, clamoured for guns and drilled for preference outside police barrack doors.

Michael Collins bent over his heaps of documents, sometimes with furrowed brow and again with transient flashes of mirth in his lively and kindly eyes. Sometimes he swore loudly and sometimes he sighed. He knew himself that he was a hard and exacting taskmaster, yes, a difficult man to work with in some moods, like a volcano one minute, with outstretched hand and apology five minutes later, when his sense of justice erupted to reproach his outbursts. Comely, too, energetic and wiry frame, strong and pallid features on which was stamped unusual determination, and in his searching gaze will and a suggestion of force in reserve.

The wars, the Great War and the Little War, had blown some spark in his soul to white-heat. And as Mick brooded over his desk in silence, Arthur Macken brooded, too, over a gallery of portraits of the man before him reconstructed from chance phrases and glimpses; the young schoolboy rambling over a southern countryside with wondering gaze beneath a peaked cap askew on a high forehead; now racing barefooted over road, slope, hill and stream, again, birds'-nesting, hurling, fighting and absorbing what mental lore he meets . . . the wanderer of sixteen years, athirst with an exile's dreams, plans, longings and experiences in the counting houses of London . . . blustering, crude, groping; but stirred to the depths by the dream of Ireland free, never so dear to the Irish than under foreign skies.

More dramatic portraits stirred and flashed in Macken's memory as he awaited the return of Sean Condron or Mick to break the silence. . . . Quick and dangerous work that night. . . . War was war . . . and yet? Without such eyes, how powerless the British Government would be . . . nearer and nearer . . . hotter and hotter . . . they or him . . . Dan or Mick, a pair of them in it. . . . Would Mick never speak?

After a glance at the Webley revolver on the table, Macken went back to his portrait gallery. No wonder Dick was piqued at being taken off the job, but Dick would find another excitement up in the hills that very evening. . . . An exile returning, clean-shaven youth in Irish Volunteer uniform . . . trials of conspiracy, insurrection, deportation . . . leadership . . . pursuit which misses him by hairs-breadths and seconds. . . . A more assured and peremptory figure—tense and mature—the intelligence and driving force behind this guerrilla war which now played round thousands of trench helmets, lorries and police barracks. . . . And his future? A feeling haunted Macken as he watched—a presentiment. Destiny of the Great who sow and do not reap, a Moses striking too impetuously on the rock and denied all else but a glimpse of the Promised Land. . . . Always so sure of himself. . . . Subtle and ambitious, no doubt. . . . Where would they be without him?

Sean Condron entered. The Tiger Doyle came close behind. Mick looked up, grave and worn as he questioned Sean. So many raids and so many arrests contemplated, so the proclamation had been issued to the evening papers? Mick relaxed and ripped out a Rabelaisian oath like a child amused with a new toy. No one could swear like Mick and no one could invest swear-words with such jollity. His eyes twinkled: gutties and louts and mangy rascals! And an answer coming to them before they were much older. . . . Oh, yes, the job, yes. Dick was raging by all accounts, but he would be a steadying influence among the rabbits and as pleased as Punch later . . . yes, all over the thirty-two counties! So much for their proclamation. Well, good luck, all three!

The three men strolled casually through the door. Michael Collins turned back to the papers before him.

.   .   .   .   .   .

Night found groups of citizens debating the proclamation in the evening papers and the raids that afternoon on the Volunteer centres and the numerous arrests.

"Old French is gathering up the poisonous insects, as he calls the lads."

"Says more than his prayers, that old bandjax, since the Germans knocked him baw-ways!"

"He can spout to the boy scouts till he bursts, but Mick will put a bee's nest in his ear."

"Ah, talk about something cheerful!"

"There's a lot coming to some people. Gob, it was a near thing for that G-man the other night——"

"I don't hold with this new picking off of bobbies——"

"Bobbies, me neck! No one ever done anything to a decent bobby in the city of Dublin yet except the criminal classes. Look at Dan Hogan beyond, grinning to himself after his smart work this day."

"The ruffian!"

And there was a smile on Dan Hogan's face as he took an evening stroll. They couldn't beat him for knowledge of the rebels and their haunts, marching at the head of a raiding party and picking out the goats from the sheep. Getting angry about it too, as his weekly mail of threatening letters showed. Balderdash and hot air! Cheek of the devil, that fellow, Mick Collins, and he had the devil's luck, always giving those Cockney tinhats the slip, and over roofs and down water-pipes in the nick of time.

Dan Hogan paused, fumbled in his pocket and handed two-pence to a beggar woman selling laces. It might get a bed in Heaven for him, poor woman . . . terrible poverty in the city of Dublin . . . and perhaps, cute and all as he was, that Collins might make a slip yet.

Turning into a dairy near at hand, Dan Hogan called for a glass of milk and chatted with the young woman at the counter. Yes, there was a new proclamation out which would put the kybosh on Mick Collins and his crowd and all the corner boys and bowsies and riff-raff who were out for trouble. The country was in a terrible state, going from bad to worse; law and order must be preserved. Politics and drink the two curses of Ireland. Good night!

The girl watched him intently as he sauntered away. A bad egg, that fellow! He would give his own father and mother up. Hadn't he pointed out Sean MacDermott and many another since? Blackguarding decent folk. Called himself an Irishman. She shrieked suddenly with involuntary terror. Three sharp reports—three vivid flashes—a cry of death and fear from outside the door. She rushed to the threshold and looked out. Three men dashed past and away into the darkness. Some hundred yards on the lights of the Dublin Central Police Station streamed out. Two burly constables on duty, watching the busy traffic rolling past a moment before, rushed up with a bewildered crowd of pedestrians. They gazed in horror at the corpse of Dan Hogan, stone-dead on the pavement. Hogan's name circulated.

"And still they want us to give them Home Rule!" said a little Cockney in the crowd, very pleased with himself.

"Coming to the bastard long enough!" said a voice in the crowd. "He looked for it."

"God rest his soul!" said one of the burly policemen who peered down into Hogan's face, all grey and still, with a lighted match. . . . Five minutes later the traffic rolled onwards again.

. . . . . .

Dermott Considine was holding, that evening, a council in the little mill among the hills. Thirty men were lined up at the lower end of the top room, gripping ashplants and rifles. The stream rippling below could be seen through the open windows. Sentries were posted on the four sides of the mill. Considine finished speaking and the men broke up into waiting groups. Dick Blake and Edward Malone, the elderly man, argued in a corner about life in Frongoch and the shrapnel which had missed them on the Post Office roof except for a flying splinter or two, and the new tides sweeping through Ireland, and the latest rumour of a gun-running. Tom Hughes spoke quietly to a dozen men in another corner, droning away monotonously, that every wall bored was a life saved, that a brick wall could resist a powerful bullet, that at a pinch a poker was as good as a pickaxe to dislodge that first resistance in the most obstinate wall, that walls must be bored zig-zag fashion in all buildings seized, or otherwise an attacking party could fire right through. . . .

"Listen to him!" said Dick Blake. "Wrapping his Easter Week mantle round him to overawe the newcomers. Seizing public buildings, I ask you, when the military occupy all our old positions as regular as the clock every Easter Week! Gob, I do dislike fellows shouting the day after the fair. What I want to know is what's in the wind tonight. Mick's up to something."

"What harm is Tom's old talk?" asked Malone.

"FALL IN! QUICK MARCH!"

The thirty men filed down the stairs and into the falling darkness up the hill slopes, Considine leading. A mile farther onwards the main road reappeared. Sharp commands split the company into two parties. Malone and Dick Blake remained with the larger body, which climbed the slopes and pressed on, higher and higher above Dublin. Underneath, a quarter of a mile away, lay the square barracks where the fat sergeant sat under his rose arch and watched the four roads. He and his six constables had done that for years. And every week the fat sergeant had sent in a bulky account of the activities of Considine and his Volunteers, thinking they were great fools to give him the trouble and with not the slightest animosity towards any of those wild fellows. Higher and higher above the slopes into the forest behind. For an hour twenty men marched and countermarched as the drill terms were shouted and Dublin grew dimmer below. In twos and threes the absent section of the company returned. Dick Blake looked at the shotguns and fowling-pieces the ten men carried and knew they had been arms-raiding. The great houses in the neighbourhood, farmers, doctors and retired colonels, had paid toll to the Invisible Army.

Dick Blake was piqued. Why had Mick taken him off the job? A man's teeth chattered in the darkness and his voice broke into a wail of fear. A curse, a hiss of laughter, the glint of a revolver, and the wail subsided. . . . So that was Mick's little game! . . . And the thick ejot in the dark had twigged it before Dick. . . . All the same, Mick might have dropped a hint. . . .

A peremptory voice called the company to attention. It was Michael Collins in uniform. His eyes gleamed in his pallid face. A homely harangue broke with power and directness on his listeners . . . a power, too, in the lilt of his Cork accent and the restless shake of his dark head . . . chaffing the man whose teeth had chattered and whose voice had wailed in fear. . . . Republican Army . . . not playing at soldiers . . . nothing but a Republic . . . men of Easter Week . . . work to be done . . . that was why they were gathering arms . . . any bloody coward present could go home now at a gallop . . . and snow to the heels of lousers like that . . . a test tonight. . . .

Again sharp orders, and the company faded down the slopes in sixes and sevens, gripping weapons and clanking petrol cans, down, down, down, to the square barracks which dominated Kilbride cross-roads.

A challenge, a wail of fear as a circle of flame and rifle-shot echoes ringed the building. . . . Again and again the shots rattled on the steel shutters. . . . A Very light darted heavenwards. Prolonged firing shook the lonely hillsides . . . the Volunteers closed in, and the circle was contracted in a series of short rushes. . . . Something crashed on the roof and a tongue of flame shot up, lighting the circle of attackers outside. . . . A white flag was thrust through an upper window. . . . The fat sergeant and his six constables threw their arms into the road and came out slowly, hands above their heads. . . . The attackers bound them and left them on the roadside. . . . Small bodies of men rushed inside the barracks and dashed petrol on the walls. . . . The sinking flames on the roof screamed to life in a red glare skywards, a howling dawn revealing the bound constables, the cross-roads, the woods and hills behind. . . . Far below shone the searchlights of a military lorry where khaki forms peered across the felled trees which blocked the main road. . . . Again the wailing voice of the man whose voice had wailed in fear before the attack, wailing now as he rolled in agony on the ground, flames playing round his petrol-soaked head and hands. . . . He was borne into the darkness moaning, while his companions mutter imprecations on his failure to obey sundry warnings whispered while the waiting circle had prepared the final rush *re* right and wrong use of petrol in demolishing enemy buildings. . . . The last dark form darted up the hill slopes, and the wailing voice died away. . . . It was a deepening of the guerrilla struggle, and its echoes were heard that night in many other counties in Ireland; the arms raid, the sudden attack, the ruined barracks and the escape of the Invisible Army. . . . Ever wider and deeper.

. . . . . .

Later that night, Macken was striding homewards, rather abstracted, a book under his arm. He encountered Michael Kerrigan, also homeward bound.

"Any news?" asked Macken.

"Do you live in the moon, man? Hogan was shot dead this evening. Begob, he was asking for it. You fellows are good shots! The man before you missed by a mile, all the same."

"Looking for it?" returned Macken pensively. "I wonder." Then he added tartly:

"If you are such a judge of marksmanship, and good G-men and bad G-men, I daresay you'll find plenty of material to practise on!"

Michael plodded serenely onward, protesting:

"Me, a judge of marksmanship? Me, a judge of G-men? Gob, the less you know and have to do with those fellows, the better, And, man, I couldn't hit a coco-nut! I'm a man of peace, and I love me country, every blade of grass."

CHAPTER IX

DAVID HARDING sat at his desk in the *Emancipator* office. Edward MacTaggart, who specialised in the more sensational news, told him of Dan Hogan's violent end that evening nearly outside the *Emancipator's* main entrance.

"Holy Gee!" MacTaggart shouted, oblivious of a pained look in the faces round the table. "Another cop has left for Heaven!" He read the message aloud.

Thomas O'Kane looked up. He came from the Falls Road, Belfast, and never forgot that MacTaggart came from Sandy Row, although Edward's sympathies were with Green rather than Orange. But Thomas O'Kane suspected the black drop in Edward's veins. He said, therefore:

"Pity they didn't get all his friends in Sandy Row!"

"Hogan was a better Papist than yourself," said Edward. "No mourning in Sandy Row for him. And if the lads wait for some tame Fenians we know to help them, they'll wait till Tibb's Eve, and you know when that is, Thomas."

After further exchanges, silenced by the intervention of the Chief, MacTaggart dashed off some lurid headings and consulted the room on them. Then, pleased with his efforts, he lay back and pointed with a grin to prominent legends on the walls:

THIS SHIP CARRIES NO PASSENGERS. WE LIVE BY LOYALTY TO THE "EMANCIPATOR." WORK LIKE HELEN B. MERRY.

Harding mechanically pursued his work, wondering to himself. Yes, people beneath the surface were shocked at the bloodshed. To some it seemed like forcing an open door. Why fire a shot when you had the country behind you? And. . . . Crushing down his swirling thoughts, he plunged into headings and manuscripts, lulled by the steady throb of the machines. The clock's hands above his head moved with incredible speed. Around the long table ten sub-editors bent over the heaps of copy and mounds of flimsies under the glare of the electric lamps. The Chief sat at the head, not yet recovered from his perusal of that morning's paper. So many misprints, so many escapes from libel, so many marches stolen from and by the *Liberator*—and if that paper had four times the circulation and three times the staff, where was the consolation in that?—so many demands from the Advertising Manager for free puffs, so many wild schemes hatched by the Editor and proprietor to be dealt with firmly, and on the spot, with a glint of the eye, and a thrust of the tongue—all this pervaded the busy room in caustic asides as the Chief smote the mountains of copy in front of him and hurled them along the table and never smiled until four in the morning as he pinned the poster on the wall and reached for his hat.

Thomas P. Bolger arrived and inquired for Papa Shanahan. He was anxious to bestow and receive sundry blacks. Michael Kerrigan, too, and the atmosphere rose to fever heat. He went, after hammering his fist on the table and looking the Chief straight in the eye. Another story mangled, another day's work botched by pseudo-aristocrats, more copy "milked," and a solemn protest to the Editor threatened. The Chief shining as a diplomat until Edward MacTaggart looked up from Michael's copy with the suggestion that it was unnecessary to use ten words where two would do, and that grammars and dictionaries were cheap. Papa Shanahan fanning the flames and Thomas O'Kane valiantly enfilading the Reporting Staff till it retired with oaths and insults, and a slam of the door that swept a gale of copy into the waste-paper baskets. . . . Hurly-burly of Press hour comes with the descent of the Chief to the "stone" to make up. Last-minute alarms and conferences, and then the music of the presses hurling thousands of new *Emancipators* to a waiting world. Morning, and Harding sets out on a solitary tramp homewards, unless the goods tram gives him a lift and he hears the woes of leader writers and printers' wisdom as the tram glides along, and for fare one copy of the *Emancipator* to the driver.

Through the winding corridors and numberless passages of the office down to the panting machines passed the national epic, in flimsy copy and with lightning speed, the national epic which rolled remorselessly onward through blood and anguish to its inexorable end. And as the national epic unrolled, journalists who had known revolutions, wars, earthquakes and all the sensational sorrows of the earth, arrived and were moved to amazement by the adventures of the *Emancipator* and its staff. It was something as follows: spasms, lulls, expectation of spasms, spasms, lulls, expectations. . . .

Every evening Harding entered the office and wielded his blue pencil while the clock's hands whirled. . . . Again there came to him that curious feeling of being a Sphinx watching the antics of short-lived desert animals.

With the whirling hands above Harding's head innumerable seconds, hours, days, months and years passed. The Black and Tans entered with a glare of "shot-up" towns in their wake . . . and Harding, to whom since Nineteen Sixteen this long epic of human suffering had become a waking nightmare and a burning obsession, set his teeth at his desk and even in the savagery of that conflict found consolation in the words of Whitman:

> *I walked the shores of my Eastern sea,*
> *Heard over the waves the little voice,*
> *Saw the divine infant where she woke mournfully wailing*
> *Amid the roar of cannon, curses, shouts, crash of*
> *   falling buildings,*
> *Was not so sick from the blood in the gutters running,*
> *Nor from the single corpses, nor those in heaps, nor*
> *Those borne away in the tumbrils,*
> *Was not so desperate at the battues of death—was not*
> *So shocked at the repeated fusillades of the guns.*
> *Pale, silent, stern, what could I say to that long-accrued*
> *Retribution?*
> *Could I wish humanity different?*
> *Could I wish the people made of wood and stone?*
> *Or that there be no justice in destiny or time?*

Two ambushes a day in Dublin. . . . Twice Harding walked in and out of the street ambushes—a memory to set nerves and heart a-jump. Lorries crawling along the streets, lumbering behind humming tram-cars and dense crowds, indistinct masses of Glengarry caps or trench helmets inside wire netting, rifles protruding. The population gulping down all the fresh air before Curfew, with its shuttered tension, night-firing and raiding.

Explosions of hurtling bombs, the sharp reports of revolvers, the retreat of the young men who had loitered so innocently around corners a moment before, heavy volleys of rifle-fire, prostrate and injured civilians, bloody and dazed and moaning and cursing, shop windows starred with bullet holes, panic, stampede and search. He remembered, too, how rarely bomb or revolver bullet found its target—going wide or falling some yards short with baffled and ominous roar. His second experience had been just like that. Two nice young fellows with a roadway and a Black and Tan lorry before them, a network of lanes in the rear for retreat. One had thrown the bomb almost over his shoulder, the other had discharged a revolver close to his ear. The shots had flown high through a plate-glass window, spattering brickwork, anywhere, everything except the huge lorry—soon one vivid flashing and roaring of rifle volleys. Down into the crowd the bomb had fallen, missing the lorry by several yards. The attackers fled with ropes round their necks to the safe retreat of the lanes and oblivious of a mild young man on the pavement shrieking with a shattered foot: "The curse of Christ on you!" And every evening this war of the streets went on, and sometimes the ropes closed round the necks of the young men, and sometimes the Black and Tans brought some dead and wounded back to barracks; but every evening the hospitals had their civilian quota, and after each ambush the military shortened the Curfew hour.

But Harding, too, had his evening of thrills in the office. The sub-editor worked under Curfew whilst heavy night-firing, soon as familiar as the throb of the printing machines, cheered the hours until dawn, and a choice selection of horrors generally composed his copy. Anonymous letters, stale from repetition, came from both sides. Sometimes on the same post an I.R.A. sympathiser promises the staff early melodrama and lurid personal possibilities for all and each. In another epistle, cheery and outspoken individuals, hiding behind the pseudonym, "Boys of the R.I.C.," are as emphatic and as unpleasant: repeated warnings having been ignored, premises and personnel are to be blown up on a given date, every bullet will find its billet, petrol may be had and matches are cheap. The aforesaid Boys hope to have the pleasure of finally wrapping the Green Flag round the *Emancipator*. "Begod, no one loves us," said Michael Kerrigan, laughing like a philosopher.

An evening came when Michael, Harding and a few printers lingered at the office entrance. Curfew hour did not fall till ten, and that was more than two hours away. Two lorries of Auxiliaries passed down the main street, some hundred yards away, and vanished from sight. All at once, two terrific explosions shook the neighbourhood, and revolver shots, followed by heavy and rapid rifle-fire, followed. A street battle seemed in progress, and the dark uniformed Auxiliaries were seen rushing, rifles in hand, along the footpaths.

"Cover, boys!" cries Michael, darting up the stairs. "A brave man never looks behind!" Inside the *Emancipator*, excitement reigns as the savage ebb and flow of rifle and revolver shots continue outside, now near, now distant. Only desultory shots are heard as the great clock swings a half-hour's circle. The Chief remembers his war service with the Greeks and rallies his quaking subs sternly: "No recruits for the wars here, I fear. On with the work." The nerve-racked staff begins to crack a few jokes; the sub-editors, with grim smiles and pallid faces, concentrate on markets, fashion notes and the generous budget provided by Papa Shanahan and his colleagues, cursing the wretched reporters who haven't sent in a line yet about the row outside. . . . The Chief waxes eloquent on misprints and issues a warning about libels and that food case—— Crash! And angry voices come up the stairs and the smashing of glass is heard below. The door is hurled violently open and every hand drops blue pencil and flimsy, remaining high in the air.

An Auxiliary, revolver in hand, has entered and summons his companions with an exultant shout. He orders everyone downstairs. "Put 'em up!" yells an excited and gaunt warrior in plain clothes, as the staff descend the winding passages to the street. But a lean and tense Auxiliary nearby countermands the order in sorrow and anger: "Put down your hands, we don't murder people in cold blood—we're not Shinners, we're British, thank God."

Armoured cars and lorries have drawn up outside. Away beyond the big grey police station fronting the *Emancipator*, and in the maze of slums in the rear, one still hears occasional gunfire. The Auxiliaries, shaken by the ambush, scowl fiercely at the neighbouring windows, evidently unnerved, but a very polite

74

young gentleman is in charge. A lady looks down on the scene from an adjoining top-storey window. A fierce shout checks itself and the Auxiliaries sweep their caps to the earth, gracious smiles lighting those rugged countenances.

A policeman peeps out of the Police Station opposite. "Put your bloody head in, you up there!" He smiles. Bang! The bullet misses the policeman by an inch. The horrified young gentleman in charge, who has been watching developments aloofly, discovers the mistake and dispatches an apology to the police.

Meanwhile, the printers have been descending the stairs in twos, a hundred strong. A bluff and grey-haired warrior in Glengarry cap, a revolver in one hand, a rifle in the other, performs feats of agility, bestowing hearty kicks on the rear of each printer emerging. His comments are personal, terse and direful. "Five minutes more for all you murderers!" yells the warrior with the excited visage in plain clothes. He wanders down the lines of waiting men, caressing the countenance of a sub-editor or printer as he goes with the muzzle of his great revolver: "Oh, you bleeding I.R.A. assassins!" he shrieks.

The young gentleman in charge intervenes and questions the staff one by one. He eyes them closely and asks:

"What do you know about this ambush?"

"What is your work in the *Emancipator*?"

"What is your name? . . . All right. . . . Go upstairs."

The raiders drive away swearing by all their gods that shots have been fired by someone in the office. Work is in full swing. Foreign correspondents look in and remain. Curfew falls, and the Editorial Department exchange views with Dublin Castle on the telephone.

A second raid follows. Auxiliaries accompanied by a military Staff Officer arrive, very indignant at the slanderous suggestion conveyed to Dublin Castle that anything extraordinary has occurred, and alternatively that shots were fired during the ambush from the office, and that it is only due to the discipline of the Auxiliaries that the bloodiest reprisals had not followed, and again that the scurrilous propaganda of the *Emancipator* was partly responsible for the lawless condition of the city, and it ought not to whine if some of its own chickens came home to roost.

"This is what we have to put up with!" storms the Staff Officer pathetically as he interrogates members of the staff, American and other correspondents in the presence of the virtuous Auxiliaries. He snaps out his questions as he summons printers, sub-editors and reporters.

"Did you see violence used on anyone here in this office tonight? Answer quick! No, of course you did not. No. You? No. Look at what we have to put up with!"

For each man questioned shook his head. And the Staff Officer would have covered the aching rears of the printers and the revolver-tapped cheeks of the sub-editors in the mantle of that not inexplicable reticence and prudence had not Michael Kerrigan started an argument on the landing with one of the new raiders. Michael was ponderous and gave that dark and bilious Auxiliary word for word. Smash! And Michael lost two teeth outside the door and confronted the astonished Staff Officer with a mouthful of blood.

"Did you see anyone——" began that persistent examiner.

"No," said Michael prudently, "I *saw* no one molested."

The Staff Officer looked at Michael and at several broken doors. He becomes less pathetic, inclines to believe that no shots have been fired from the office, examines the British Army commission the Managing Editor shakes indignantly in his face, accepts a drink of whiskey in token of peace and departs in a more mellow and judicial frame of mind.

"I am a man of peace," said Michael Kerrigan. "But I hope those beauties walk into the boys some dark night. . . . Knights of the Pen like us, though, suffer and do as much for our country as any gunman of them all—and no one loves us!"

CHAPTER X

IT was David Harding's night off. He mounted his bicycle and pedalled towards the hills. The message he had read the previous night, and which had been crowded out of that morning's papers, still haunted him. Edward MacTaggart had tossed it aside. Six lines. It read: "Mrs. Lavelle, an elderly woman, belonging to a well-known County Cork family, has been missing for some days, and her absence is causing her relatives some anxiety."

"Anyone know the Lavelles?" asked the Chief, screwing his eyes at the flimsy and tapping his forehead. "Yes, yes, let me think. They were strong Unionists and landlords and unpopular in the Land League times. Give it a small head, MacTaggart, to be on the safe side. But Cork has been filling the blood column this last week, hasn't it, Harding? Had enough of it? Well, do markets tomorrow. Nothing like contrast. You have that seedy 'blood column' look. What? The R.I.C. man, who resigned, writes to our local correspondent to deny report that unknown men entered his house and soundly flogged him and wants prominence given to this denial? Give him the prominence. Suppose he thought of the denial with a Black and Tan revolver pressed tightly to his head. Boy! Give this pile of bilge to the Advertising Manager, if he is still in his room. And tell him with my compliments that I have read his urgent note, and that if he expects a column puff for a two-inch ad. on a night like this, would he please go to the devil?"

"Yes, sir!" cried a pale youth, vanishing through the door and nearly colliding with Papa Shanahan.

"Shanahan," cried the Chief eagerly, "do you know the Lavelles? You, a Munster man, should be an authority on Southern families. An old lady of that name has been missing in County Cork for some days. Did you hear anything when you were down for the executions last week?"

"Give me a match, someone," said Papa Shanahan, waving his pipe and wrinkling his brow. "Thanks. Yes, I know them well. A strong landlord and Ascendency family. Old Mrs. Lavelle lived in a cottage somewhere ten miles beyond Cork City, near the scene of that ambush a month ago. Mrs. Lavelle was a stubborn old dame. She would fly the Union Jack and give out her views on strong government. Oh, a fierce old one, who was always getting threatening letters, and when her friends told her a shut mouth catches no flies, she'd round on them——"

"A two-line head to that story, MacTaggart," said the Chief. "Go on, Shanahan."

"And say: 'Shopkeepers' caution. I come of good old military stock!' Now you mention it, I did hear some talk of her when I was down, but it was vague, and exactly what it was I disremember. I put no pass on it."

"The Black and Tans had better look to their laurels!" cried Edward MacTaggart, throwing down a long type-written document. "This gives me the creeps. Military report on the I.R.A. reprisals for the executions. Ugh! Five soldiers for the six executions. Details of each. One poor devil caught going across fields after his friends had warned him not to venture."

"All lies!" snorted Thomas O'Kane. "It is the black drop in yourself that makes you squirm."

Papa Shanahan intervened:

"It's fellows sitting on their backsides in the Castle and elsewhere, trimming up facts, that causes half the wars of this world. Like the sub who murders the reporters' copy and gets the cash and credit. But that yarn is true. I know. I was down. They are half-mad in those parts, and they get a lot of moral support from lads, the like of who dug up their gardens during Easter Week and fired off their mouths when it was all over. Pity some parties don't get a gun in their paw and talk less."

"Enough, Shanahan!" said the Chief. "You and I had the sense to get our wars over young."

Papa Shanahan laid his voluminous copy before the Chief, elaborately explained it, and departed in clouds of smoke. He winked meaningly at Harding as he passed and whispered: "Are you coming out to make a statement in the interval? I'll be beyond in the 'Diamond Bar.' I'd like to see you." Harding nodded. The Chief buried himself in a mountain of copy which was soon transformed into little hills in front of each sub-editor. Michael Kerrigan came and went after a furious argument with Edward MacTaggart. The machines droned away below. The clock swept in its unrelenting circle. There was a lull, and Harding strolled across to the "Diamond Bar." Laughing groups of journalists chatted and joked. Then Papa Shanahan arrived.

"I am damned droughty. A pint." They sat at a small table. "Here's health!" Papa Shanahan downed his pint and rose with determination in his eye. "The same again, Ned!" And then he opened a conversation with the air of a man avid to relieve his mind of a burden.

"Look here. I am afraid there is a lot behind that Lavelle yarn the Chief mentioned. I have a suspicion, but I didn't want to set the Chief off on any wild-goose chase. You remember the six young fellows caught red-handed preparing an ambush? It comes back to me now. I was watching in front of the jail in Cork the morning they were executed. In batches of two. Relatives waiting outside. An interval of half an hour between each pair. Tommies and armoured cars and curses and prayers, all mixed up. A voice next my ear said bitterly: 'Sean wouldn't be going to Heaven this morning only his heart was too bloody soft.' We heard the second volley then, and the soldiers shouting to the crowd: 'Don't go home you ——s, there's two more blighters to go yet.' So the first remark went out of my mind. I had looked back at the voice, and I saw the maddest two eyes I have ever seen since I came back from Flanders. A rough lad who'd murder you if he felt fed-up on a wet day.

"But I did hear before I came back to Dublin that someone had informed the military, or rather the Black and Tans. Now the spot where the ambush was planned is on a lonely part of the main road to Cork. And old Mrs. Lavelle, it comes back to me, used to drive in fairly often to Cork. A mile beyond the spot and her house on the Cork side is a big constabulary barracks. If she saw them preparing the ambush and got through, she would have informed the police—she was that sort. Now, Sean Gibbons, who was shot, as our wild friend put it, 'for being too bloody soft,' was the leader of all the ambushes in a neighbouring area. He didn't know her reputation as well as the local lads. Ten to one, and adding what we know to what's happened, Mrs. Lavelle told Sean Gibbons some fool yarn, a sick neighbour, and she was going for a doctor. I think I heard as much. And she's vanished. Well, I wouldn't give the froth of this pint for her life this minute!"

"Nonsense!" said Harding. "The I.R.A. don't shoot women. It's notorious that they warn them to leave the country. Only last week one o' Michael Collins's men told me that Collins had issued strict orders that a woman on the North Side of the city was not to be molested. And ten men's lives may hang on her evidence."

"In Dublin," agreed Papa Shanahan, "but in the South, well, you have to live there to understand. Neither side has any sentiment. I was in the Great War myself, though it's problematical whether I ever hurt any Germans, and I have reported some very hot elections, and I'm not easily shocked—but for sheer venom and war lust give me the South this minute. Do you know anyone with the ear of Mick Collins? He might stop the funeral, but he'll have to be damned quick. Not that I've any love for the nosy old faggot, but a woman's a woman! What price 'no son of Erin will do thee harm'? Another pint, and I must be off."

Harding returned to his desk with knitted brow. Why should he interfere, as Papa Shanahan had hinted? Michael Collins would know a good deal more already of the case than anyone else. "Mind your own business!" said one voice inside him. "Don't make a fool of yourself!" said another. His reactions to the executions returned to his mind. Six shot like that. And the murderous thrill that had possessed him when he read that the Volunteers had turned out that night, and shot right and left at sight. A great fight Cork was putting up. She would—— She would not—— On a sudden impulse he determined to lay the matter before Michael Collins. And the Chief indirectly aided this impulse by calling him aside as he was leaving.

"Do me a favour," said the Chief. "The eternal friction about the holiday list has started. It's a bit early for you, but if you agree to start tomorrow, I could preserve the peace. Do you object?"

The Chief was surprised to find that Harding did not object, as he had planned a cycling tour, and his bicycle had returned only that morning renovated for the trip. After getting some money from the cashier next morning, he completed his preparations and turned his bicycle towards the hills in the early evening.

Tom Hughes hailed him at the entrance to the mill. Overhead the men were drilling, drilling, drilling, while Sean Condron shouted orders and the rafters quivered. Considine was talking earnestly in a corner to Dick Blake. Through the open windows Harding saw the familiar scene, the little stream and the glorious hills he had seen so often on the eve of Nineteen Sixteen. He told Considine his business.

"Mick will be back at Havensfield in an hour. Tell him if you like. I am going there now. But I expect he knows and has taken action already."

Along the white wide hedge-lined roads with elms and pines crowding the slopes above, they went to Havensfield, up the winding wooded avenue and into Considine's study. And Harding thought as he seated himself that the room was an eloquent index to the owner's personality. In Considine's features there was a suppressed power, a magnetism, tempered by an expression of austerity. Recluse, dreamer, fighter—it was stamped upon his desk, his book-cases, the heaped-up mass of papers which overflowed writing-tables and floor. There was a bust of Tone on the white Bossi mantelpiece, over which hung a picture of the youthful Napoleon. Quaint old prints and modern paintings of the Gaelic heroic school, with some racing sketches by Jack B. Yeats. There was a heap of MS., bearing corrections in his firm and rounded handwriting, on one writing-table.

A bookish man, one surmised, who had the vision, and, it might be added, the carelessness of the seer. He was ruled by an instinctive judgement which did not often betray him. Scrupulously tidy in his personal appearance, his study was too often the confused mass of papers Harding now saw. With an intense love of books went a disregard for his personal property in them. Considine was extremely well versed in Irish and general literature. Harding's eyes greedily devoured the titles in the rows of glass-shuttered book-cases which ran round the walls of the room. A feast to sate the most epicurean scholar or bibliophile. But he wished Considine would keep those treasures of two ancient peoples and two modern ones under lock and key and in better order.

Away on the distant heather-covered splendour, the sun sank under the hills, lighting the room with eerie grandeur—playing for a last time on the furniture's antique curves.

Michael Collins entered suddenly. He listened to Harding quietly—his eyes alert, his mouth set. He drew a pocket case from the breast of his coat, consulted some papers, nodded, went swiftly to the door and shouted:

"You, there, tell Tiger Doyle to come up at once."

He questioned Harding again. What was the mad fellow Shanahan mentioned like? Oh, yes, damn, the sleepy bunglers! Did Harding say he was on holiday at present? No late news? "It's not often," he went on smiling, "that the Press is ahead of my Intelligence Service. Glad you told me. You have stopped a tragedy, I hope. But for one fact you mentioned I shouldn't worry. And that fact, which is neither here nor there, comes to this. Sometimes men get out of hand. This is what happened. Mrs. Lavelle did inform the police. She had been warned time and again. She surprised the preparations for the ambush. At first, Gibbons ordered her to return to her house, and then threatened to arrest her. Pity he didn't, God rest his soul and the souls of the five others she gave into the clutches of the Black and Tans. Then she told him that she was driving for a doctor for a dying neighbour and worked on his feelings. He let her go. She went straight to the barracks, and then Black and Tans swooped in force and caught Gibbons red-handed."

"She was courageous," answered Harding.

"No!" said Michael Collins fiercely. "She was not courageous, but stupid. She had all the accursed arrogance of her anaemic little Ascendency caste. I would shoot her myself in the morning if she were a man. I am going to shoot her out of Ireland back to the people she's loyal to, to those who planned this Terror, and if she's wise, she'll stay out. You're wise to stick to the pen, your heart is too soft, and your brain is too mushy since Nineteen Sixteen. You believe, or think you believe, that we could win without violence and force and bloodshed. You would change your mind quick if you had half an hour's responsibility in this struggle. You would have made Gibbons's mistake. Do you know Kipling?

81

Men who spar with Government need to back their blows
Something more than ordinary journalistic prose.

Considine was about to speak when the Tiger Doyle came in.
Michael Collins rattled orders at him. He was to start for
Cork County at once on the fast motor without, and deliver
instructions for Mrs. Lavelle's release and deportation.

The Tiger roared at Michael Collins:

"War is war! If people won't mind their own business after
warning, let them take the consequences. The French and Germans shot women. Time we did. Your Intelligence Officers are
mad enough about the North Side lassie you won't let us touch.
Drop her in the bloody Liffey, and don't ask me to break my
neck to save that old she-devil and interfering bitch in County
Cork——"

"ORDERS ARE ORDERS, YOU LOUSER!"

The Tiger quailed. Michael Collins shook his dark hair and
shouted:

"I'm going to present no Nurse Cavells to the British to please
any Dublin gutty of the whole pack of you, nor let any cut-
throat in Cork County or in creation trample on my orders.
Off with you, you jumped-up son of a bitch, and none of your
old guff! On the motor as fast as you can through the dark.
Harding's going with you. Report here in ten minutes' time."

Harding started. Michael Collins grinned and spoke:

"You caused all this uproar. You are on holiday and look
sick around the gills and a tour among the lads will do you good.
Besides, I'd like to have a representative of mine with the Tiger
on this trip. His heart isn't in peaceful missions. He'll drop
you at your place on the way."

An hour later the Tiger Doyle and Harding were dashing
through the night to Cork. Towns and villages whizzed past
them, the great car howling as the Tiger drove at top speed in
silence, his eyes fixed on the road ahead, his rough firm hands
on the steering wheel. Twice a sentry's voice challenged them,
and shots sounded behind them, but the car roared on and on.
Darkness lifted, but the Tiger's eyes were as keen in the coming
morning light. At dawn they reached an isolated farmhouse in
County Cork. Harding awakened from a half-doze with a start.
The Tiger left the car in an outhouse, tumbled and ramshackle,
where Harding noticed a dilapidated Ford with much-patched
tyres. The Tiger rapped on the front door, shouting aloud.
Terence O'Donovan opened the door. Inside stood five men
with rifles in their hands and bandoliers across their shoulders.
The Tiger saluted and handed Terence O'Donovan a note.

Terence O'Donovan read the note and said tersely:

"Your drive has been for nothing, Tiger Doyle. Mrs. Lavelle is dead at the bottom of a deep bog-hole as full of lead as Sean Gibbons, and her cottage is a black ruin. Tell Mick we did our best to stop it. But——" He shrugged his shoulders.

"The Devil!" said Harding. "Is that the way you fight down here? A woman of more than sixty."

"Easy for you fellows up in Dublin to talk!" snapped Terence O'Donovan. "I am not defending this, mind, but men get out of hand and passions boil over when we have to endure what we face every hour of the twenty-four down here." He smiled bitterly and added:

"When the British make similar excuses, they are quite right!"

A bright-eyed little man laid down his rifle and said quickly:

"We know what Mick Collins and the Dublin leaders think. If it had been in our area we'd have kidnapped the old one and kept her where she'd do no harm, and we'd never have trusted her in the first instance. But Sean Gibbons came in fresh to the district, and the only lad in the ambush party who could have told him the truth foolishly kept his tongue quiet. There's a wild mad company Commandant, a friend of Sean Gibbons, who's above stairs now. He saw red after the executions and took action on his own. Wait till you see him and you'll understand. Glad you're here, Tiger Doyle. Time we offered you a bit to eat. We were on the job last night and left our mark on the Tans, and unfortunately two of our best lads behind. Great pep in the Tans, man. Though not so much as when they came down here first. Yerrah, they fight till they drop, man. But we've taken some of the sauce out of them. They don't give a damn for anything except whiskey and fighting."

The meal passed in silence. Harding noticed tell-tale wrinkles and circles on the faces of the Volunteers. The bright-eyed little man led him upstairs. Through a closed door he heard a deep Cork voice raving. Sometimes drill terms were shouted: "Form fours, about turn, two deep, as you were, stand easy." Then a wail came into the deep lilt: "Sean Gibbons, where is Sean Gibbons? Dead as bloody mutton, because he was too bloody decent and too bloody soft. Sean Gibbons, where is Sean Gibbons, the best friend I ever had? Why did he trust that bitter old pill?" Then the lilting drill orders, a long scream: "Take your hands off me! I can see her white face. She's everywhere. Her eyes. Eyes, eyes, eyes. Sinking into the bloody bog-hole as dead as Sean Gibbons. And her house is burning, burning, burning." The scream sank to low moans, and then

83

suddenly rose to savage yelps, and a flow of oaths and curses.

"He's like that all day and best part of the night," said the bright-eyed little man. "Oh, he'll get better. I've seen and heard worse than him. 'Twasn't this business alone set him off. He's been through a lot, like all the lads. Come in and look at him."

Through the opened door Harding saw a stout dark man, and two others holding him down. His face was white and distorted. Saliva streamed from his lips, and in his black rolling eyes were reflected a thousand rages and hatreds and despairs. He glared at Harding and shrieked:

"Why did you take away my revolvers? That fellow's a spy. He'll give us away. You're all too soft, soft, soft like poor Sean Gibbons. Her eyes, her eyes, her bloody eyes everywhere. O Agonising Christ!"

Then he hid his face in the pillows and moaned and wept. Terence O'Donovan came in and sat beside the bed. The man fell into a deep sleep, and the watchers stole away, leaving the bright-eyed little Volunteer on guard.

Harding was sensitive to atmosphere. Already he could feel the pressure of the guerrilla war, and its effects on the fleeting fugitive fighters, and the mass of the people. Each second was filled with a terror and a tenseness. The first night he walked to a small neighbouring town on the Cork road. As he and the Tiger Doyle entered, they heard lorries on the road behind them, and looking round again noticed three lorry-loads of troops, accompanied by an armoured car.

The Tiger went into the house to which Terence O'Donovan had directed them, and watched through the front windows. The lorries and armoured car rushed through at full speed. The Tiger shook his head thoughtfully and led the way upstairs. The house was empty, and the Tiger seemed lost in thought. "We might sleep better in yon farmhouse," he said, "in spite of the mad fellow's howls. Terry and Co. are on the job again tonight. Only for that damned night drive I would have taken a hand myself."

An hour passed, but neither the Tiger nor Harding could sleep. They sat at the darkened windows, talking in whispers and smoking. The Tiger pointed out the police barracks a few doors away, and smiled. "Mick always stays. Hides next door to a barracks for preference. It's safer." He looked out and pronounced the place a nice little town.

"Look at the factory yonder, and the two fine rows of shops. Oh, here's the police patrol. Let's turn in."

Silence fell over the streets, and not a light could be seen in the main thoroughfare. The two men retired to rest, and sank into a heavy sleep. Some hours passed. All at once Harding awoke. Away in the distance he heard continued fusillading. The Tiger slept on. The shots in the distance died away. The noise of a motor engine grew louder and nearer. Harding peered through the windows.

Below a military lorry dashed past. As it did the soldiers within fired repeated volleys in the air. A second lorry followed, and a third. The soldiers jumped down yelling wildly, and a smashing of glass was heard. In the darkness a red glare showed and flames rose from the small factory. Blue uniformed men rushed from the police barracks and pleaded with the angry troops. Officers shouted at the maddened men, but the wild scene went on. Volley after volley was discharged in the air.

The Tiger Doyle was on his feet. He whispered to Harding:

"I knew there would be trouble and reprisals. The Lavelle business and the two ambushes. Look, some of this lot have been wounded. They've broken loose. But it's not from that quarter the worst of the trouble will come."

The shouting officers at last herded the infuriated troops to the lorries, and with a burst of angry songs they drove away. The townspeople dashed out and extinguished the fire with buckets and hoses.

Early next morning a motor-car drove into the main street, and Thomas P. Bolger and Michael Kerrigan descended, waving notebooks in a business-like fashion. They stayed half an hour and interviewed the parish priest, the police and twenty townspeople, including the leading merchant, who wrung his hands over the damage to his hotel and two stores and cursed the wild young men who had started all the trouble and led the military to destroy his treasures. Thomas P. Bolger was heard shouting to Kerrigan as they drove off:

"Hard lines on the old cod, Michael, and he so down on the gunmen."

"Hard lines, indeed—the richest old huckster in these parts, and still loyal to the Party."

Early that evening three tenders dashed into the town and a cry rose: "The Black and Tans!" Shouting shapes rushed through the streets, firing revolvers, and again the crash of glass was heard, and fiercer and more fatal flames roared round the now doomed factory. Through the night the Tiger and Harding watched—helpless spectators. Stones crashed through the windows and the flames leaped and howled as the factory swayed

85

and collapsed. Panic and women's screams and the constables from the barracks shouting to the Black and Tans: "Leave that house alone, can't ye? They're quiet decent people. . . ." At dawn the raiders drove away with a final orchestral flourish of revolvers and rifles. And Harding and the Tiger Doyle saw the charred factory and six ruined houses, mere shells, the iron bedsteads twisted to fantastic moulds by the heat. Women stole back, with mad despairing broken looks in their eyes to hover whimpering near their former homes: "Devils, devils, devils! Did you ever hear or see such devils, devils, devils?"

A mile away, Terence O'Donovan and twenty Volunteers waited in ambush. As the three tenders rounded the bend the road was shaken with the earthquake of a landmine exploding, the rattle of rifles and the bursting of grenades. . . . One tender dashed ahead—a flaming chariot of spitting rifles as it went, with six wild-faced shrieking crew, towards Cork with two dead men across the sides. The second tender capsized into the gaping hole the landmine had blown in the road and burst into flames. From the third tender came the rattle of rifles and revolvers and grenades hurled madly towards the roadside, and the savage and regular volleys which poured into the tender from there. The air was shaken by explosion after explosion. A roar and humming of motors floated down on the breeze. But too late to save the Black and Tans, who threw down their arms and held their hands above their heads. They were surrounded, trussed and left on the roadside. With a final volley in the direction of the approaching lorries, Terence O'Donovan and his men faded away with the arms and equipment of the Auxiliaries, leaving the burning tenders, six dead and six wounded on the blackened and blood-soaked grass. . . .

  . . . .

A week later, Terence O'Donovan sent word to the Tiger Doyle and Harding to return to the farmhouse, as the column had returned, and Michael Collins had sent orders for the Tiger to join it in company with Arthur Macken. It was with regret that the Tiger Doyle obeyed, for he and Harding had wandered through the restful spots of County Cork among the men "on the run" and into the hiding-places of the Invisible Army. They listened at nights around camp-fires in the hills to many wild and sad tales of the times, and met again men they had not seen since the days in Frongoch. The Tiger listened with inexhaustible interest to all tales of the Press. He thought Harding a fool to lead such a life, and offered him a place in his

column any time sense and a normal outlook returned to him:
"Not that you would be any bloody use, David, but you're
good company!"

Arthur Macken was waiting in the little lonely farmhouse
when they went back, and the wild Commandant had departed,
cured of his hysteria. They visited the charred cottage of Mrs.
Lavelle, guided by the bright-eyed little Volunteer. Four walls
remained. A shell merely, and within an iron bedstead, twisted
into the same fantastic shape as those in the "shot-up" town
when the women had stolen back with despair in their eyes.
. . . But to Harding the place was still haunted by an imperious
old lady. She seemed to wander round rigid and unconquered,
dusting her windows, judging her neighbours, reading with simple
faith and satisfaction the firm leading articles in papers of her
colour, the *Irish Times* with Latin quotations and phrases sacred
to her from childhood, the full-throated baying of the *Morning
Post,* the infallible, rolling, acidulous periods of *The Times*,
hanging out her Union Jack—alive in her narrow and bitter
dreamland, avid to defend the lands and sway of the Southern
Ascendency, with the same germ in her brain that had raved
and gibbered in the farmhouse's upper room.

"Great fight in that old one, God rest her soul!" said the
bright-eyed little Volunteer. "She told me once there would
never be peace in Ireland until we were all strung up on
trees."

"Do you know the old legend of St. Brigit, a Tory pamphleteer
made?" asked Harding. "It fits this case. Her angel told her
that in Ireland, of all Western lands, souls fell into Hell as quick
as a hail shower, for in Ireland 'is most continual war, root of
hate and envy, and of vices contrary to charity.' "

"Easy for angels to talk like that," said the little Volunteer.
"If the English Terror drives some of us mad, there's many a
woman breaking her heart today for the sons she won't see
again or stretched under the clay like the poor young one who
got the contents of a rifle in her belly in Galway last week, and
she going to have a baby. An accident, I grant you. A careless
Tommy. But none the less sad for that."

Macken asked bitterly, with a hard glint in his eyes: "What
would you? These Southern Ascendency are all the same. Not
one of them has spoken a brave or helpful word since this Little
War started. Till we burned their mansions when the military
destroyed houses and shops as a reprisal for the ambushes down
here, they never spoke a word against the Terror. They are
a traitor colony. They would all give us away, and gloat over

our executions, if they had Mrs. Lavelle's courage. They have neither the guts of the English nor their guile!"

"No," said the little Volunteer. "You are wrong there, Arthur, I have slept under their roofs when they had only to give the wink to the raiding lorry some doors way. You forget the white in our flag. Peace between Orange and Green. Didn't the Ascendency give us Tone and Mitchel and Davis and Parnell? And Hyde, who saved the Irish language? But since the trouble started we have forgotten all those things, and we'll pay dear for it some day if we are not careful. Half the young fellows who are coming into our movement haven't the grounding of the men who started the Sinn Fein movement. Irish history they learn at public meetings, and the Irish language they learn on posters, and they are out for excitement, and never look ahead."

"We might try a little Christianity," said Harding aloud, looking again on the haunted cottage with the imperious old lady, dusting her windows, and wandering in her rigid circle, her fierce old eyes defying the world.

"That's the talk!" said the little Volunteer. "When we've knocked some more lard out of the Tans. A baptism of fire for those fellows!"

So talking, they returned to the cottage. Leaving the Tiger Doyle behind him, Harding returned to Dublin. When he told his tale at Havensfield, Michael Collins sighed and shrugged his shoulders. Considine turned back to his books with sadness in his eyes.

CHAPTER XI

ONE Saturday morning, Dick Blake was very puzzled by a brief note from Sean Condron. Sean, the temperate member, the second Father Matthew, the quiet young fellow making an urgent appointment for that evening in a public-house! It was true that the public-house was Thomas O'Dea's, and Sean in his note suggested that the meeting was not to be a convivial one. But Sean's previous visits there had been on rare occasions to Thomas's upper room. In this note Sean was explicit: the bar no less! Sean in a bar, Sean who preached cold water and the beauties and duties of temperance until his company groaned, Sean whose propaganda and airs on the subject were insufferable. Dick read the note again with fire in his eye. And all the curious glances the young one at home gave him while he read it! A fly couldn't walk into the house but the smallest and the youngest of the women started their eternal, provoking and inescapable questions. And he had told the truth: a night with the boys in Sean Condron's company, a pub crawl plus an eloquent porter-illustrated lecture on prohibition by one who knew both sides, and had at last found that man does not live by water alone, and, of course, that set the young one off with sour looks and testimonials to Sean's example in these matters and a sermon on the fit and proper behaviour for a man of his years and responsibilities. As good as her dead mother, begod. . . . Dick re-read the note and groaned: worse and worse. Amateur sleuthing! Fishes ready to chase whales and fly in the face of sharks. So much for temperance! Long-faced good boys, who never smoked or took a glass or gave the world the weight of their tongues now and again, always had a screw loose somewhere. Well, Sean should have the weight of his tongue, and Mick should hear about it, and Sean should go home footless and back teeth floating even if he tried the dry-ginger racket. More looks from the young one and acid words and questions. Dividing families, these namby-pamby tea-and-bun fanatics! So out with Dick Blake, pondering deeply.

On his return in the evening, Dick oiled his revolver in the most ostentatious manner, dressed himself in his Sunday best, handed over the household money to his little daughter, May, and told her that there was a special mobilisation at the mill, and that he would not return until Sunday night at the earliest.

Sean Condron was waiting near the Custom House. He, too, was spick and span. He was turning towards Thomas O'Dea's when Dick addressed him in firm and vigorous tones:

"Look a-here, Mr. Bloody Sean Condron. The movement is the movement, and in that you are supreme, but in certain matters you are a child. As long as I have known you, I have had to endure your antics and self-righteousness on a certain subject. One word is as good as ten. Is it your intention to play the sleuth within? That's my job. Because a simple slob of a polisman straight from the bog'd have you taped a mile away. You'd be worse within than the only teetotaller ever known on the *Emancipator*, a most conscientious young fellow Harding was telling me about only last week. They sent him to the Black North to worm the secrets out of the Orangemen after some riot or pogrom in those parts. He stood them all dry gingers—the beverage of cravens!—like a lord, and he was carried back to Dublin in splints just after he entered the second boozer in Sandy Row——"

Sean Condron wrinkled his brows, but said disarmingly: "Oh, I'm in your hands, Dick. Don't worry, my dear fellow. I only want to meet someone Mick said might be there. Isn't there one of those quiet railed-off places inside?"

"A snug, you mean," answered Dick, mollified. "Several of them, and the safest place for strangers like yourself. But what's this Sunday suit and revolver idea? On principle, I never discuss the movement within, not even in a snug, and I never expected to have to remind you of that! Holy boys like yourself never know where to draw the line."

Condron leaned forward and whispered half a dozen words in Dick's ear. Dick shrugged his shoulders, looked thoughtful for a moment, and then waved his hands in indifferent agreement. The two men went into a lonely snug near the door. Thomas O'Dea's voice was booming over the tumult. Dick ordered two pints and placed one ostentatiously before Sean. Condron shuddered and pushed the tumbler towards Dick. Then he forgot his surroundings and gazed keenly through the opening over the counter into the main bar. He studied the man nearest to view, a coarse-faced solitary figure, reading a paper, tensely wrapt in an unhappy atmosphere of memory, flint and strain clashing in two fierce blue eyes. Condron nodded to himself. Dick's small talk rattled on. Condron rose and called through the snug windows in a loud aggressive voice:

"Two more bloody pints! And don't keep us here all night!"

The occupants of the bar turned in amazement, for Sean's voice carried above the babble and din. Thomas O'Dea's rubicund face, with uneasy startled eyes, appeared and loomed in the aperture. He cried in surprise:

"Sean Condron! I didn't expect the honour of your company."

"Oh," said Sean, in hilarious and thunderous tones. "Dick's leading me astray at last. And Mick was asking for you, Thomas, me old segoosher, Mick Collins, the lad the bloody Castle can't catch, and never will, and he's dropping in later." A stage whisper: "And perhaps he won't go home till morning." Sean winked and raised his voice again: "Two pints quick. Our tongues are hanging out. We can't live without it."

Dick Blake stirred uneasily. Sean was showing an unexpected side to his character. Thomas O'Dea, with a troubled look, went away and returned with two pints. Sean placed them on the table and snarled in Dick's ear: "Touch another drop and I'll plug you, so help me, God!" And raising his voice, he sang lustily:

Where is the Irishman who ever was afraid?
Where is the Irishman who wouldn't draw his blade?
To fight for King and country,
Like a hero of old?

The solitary figure rose and went swiftly out, a pallor in his
cheeks and excitement in his blazing eyes. Harding, entering,
collided with him. Muttering apologies, the stranger rushed by.
Condron's voice broke out afresh:

O you lads that are witty from famed Dublin city,
And you that in pastime take any delight,
To Donnybrook fly, for the time's drawing nigh
When fat pigs are hunted and lean cobblers fight;
When maidens, so swift, run for a new shift;
Men, muffled in sacks, for a shirt they race there;
There jockeys well booted, and horses sure-footed,
All keep up the humours of Donnybrook Fair.

He nodded gaily to Harding at the counter, beckoned to him
with his eyes, and thundered ahead:

Brisk lads and young lasses can there fill their glasses
With whiskey and send a full bumper around;
Jig it off in a tent till their money's all spent
And spin like a top till they rest on the ground.
Oh, Donnybrook capers, to sweet catgut-scrapers,
They bother the vapours, and drive away care;
And what is more glorious—there's naught more uproarious—
Huzza for the humours of Donnybrook Fair!

Dick Blake growled reproachfully: "I never would have
thought it of you, Sean, acting the bloody stage-Irishman, and
the work that's before you! If you don't stop, I'll go home."

Harding joined them, staring dumbfounded at Sean, who subsided as Thomas O'Dea again appeared. Sean whispered to
him, and Thomas O'Dea's face cleared.

"Mick's a deep lad," he said. "I'll be able for them. I had,
I can tell you, Sean, the gravest doubts of that customer, Fred
Hemp, the mad medical who joined the Army. If I had a penny
for every time I heaved him out in the old days, I'd retire tomorrow and set up the rest of you for life into the bargain."

Thomas was called away. Condron asked Harding shortly if
he knew anything about Hemp.

"I thought he was dead, killed in the war, until I saw him

91

here again lately. But what's your little game, Sean? You made me open my eyes this night!"

Condron shrugged his shoulders: "You know Thomas hides the lads from time to time? Mick has just captured a report about Thomas, a bit too accurate for Mick's taste. Mick must be sure. He makes no mistakes either way, and as he has the devil's own sense of perverted humour, he bullied and cajoled me into being his bait—sacrificing my reputation for the cause. He said that only an absolute teetotaller like myself could make the public exhibition he wanted."

"Hemp's harmless," said Harding. "And if he swallows that bait, he's a fool——"

"They're all fools," said Dick. "You'd know them a mile away, and they'd lap up the bloodiest rubbish you could tell them."

"Any sensations?" asked Harding.

"We'll read them all in the *Emancipator*," said Dick with a ponderous guffaw—significant to Harding's sensitive ear. Sean rapped the bench beside him with quick irritable movements. Dick's hand was shooting defiantly towards the three untasted pints before him when Condron glanced at his watch and muttered: "An hour till Curfew." He snapped at Dick: "Remember the morning." Outside he conducted Dick to a sidecar, saying he might see Harding on the morrow. "Three whistles from the back garden," he added. "Leave your window open."

Harding strolled homewards, thinking deeply about Michael Collins, the impish streak in him, and his hourly struggle with the espionage of the Castle. Spies everywhere, from the semi-derelict hawker to the jolly commercial traveller spouting treason and revolution to Michael Collins's own agents, Mick, whose eyes and ears caught every move and counter-move in every barracks in Ireland, the lowest whispers in Dublin Castle, the very hours the oft-baffled raiders stole out to capture Mick and find him gone. Unseen fingers copied confidential reports for Mick, unseen hands stopped the barbed barriers thrown around whole areas to entrap him sleeping—and he slept peacefully a yard away. And tonight Mick was weighing Hemp in the balance, and Heaven alone knew whom and what else.

He went into his ground-floor back bed-sitting-room, and looked out at the Drumcondra trees. Sleep deserted him, and he turned to his books, as often when the mood seized him on a Saturday night. But between the pages and his attention sounded again Dick Blake's laugh, Dick Blake the crack shot,

Dick Blake who would no more scruple to shoot a spy than to light his pipe. Hemp, pitiable victim, Hemp, who had turned as red as a child caught stealing jam and turned tail when he had met his former Volunteer Commandant in College Green in a hold-up before his demobilisation—yes, scarlet with confusion, Hemp had let the much-wanted man slip past! Perhaps that explained Mick's cat-and-mouse tactics. Hemp's face flickered between him and the page. He closed the book. Cat and mouse. . . . Always must be sure. . . . Impish, too . . . Thomas O'Dea. . . . Sleep stole over Harding at the open window.

A distant volley awakened him. The early-morning sun was shining into the room. Away, far, he heard the faint but persistent echoes of revolver shots. He turned in, but could not sleep. Half an hour passed. A low whistle sounded from the garden, three times, Sean's signal. A whisper, a form darkening the window, and Condron stepped in—pale and exhausted. He sank on the bed still panting for breath. . . . He fainted. Harding threw water on his face and opened his collar. Condron opened his eyes and drank a glass of whiskey at a gulp that Harding poured out. He looked away citywards with a melancholy and determined expression.

"All in the day's work!" he said. Then he added with a sad humour: "All the sensations you want today, Harding!"

"Wrong again," said Harding, "Sunday off for me, and the match this afternoon."

"Good, I'll come too," said Condron, all at once himself again. "Let me rest a bit. Dick will be here soon." He turned over and his eyes closed. Harding was not insensitive to an excitement outside. All Dublin's tension permeated the quiet street. Noon came, and Condron's sleep was deeper, albeit troubled. From time to time, a groan, a word, a sigh escaped from the sleeping man. One struck. A knock, and Dick's voice in the hall. "No, Mrs. Brownbill, but there's ructions down town. The Black and Tan lorries are on the move. They say there's been shootings all over the city. Sixteen court-martial officers and Intelligence men dead in their beds in hotels and houses. So I heard." A chill passed over Harding and a darkness. In spite of the columns of horror he "subbed," in spite of his sympathies, in spite of his hatred of the prowling agents and spies, this horror of bloodshed and the guerrilla weapon never died within him. And soon Dick Blake was explaining why Condron was sleeping the sleep of exhaustion.

"We slept at Sean's house near the mill, and the Tiger dropped us in the city just after Curfew lifted. About eight, several smart

93

young lads met us. I knew what was in the wind. Sean gave the word last night outside the Custom House just before we met you. One of his crack shots had been laid by the heels on Friday. So I was called in at a moment's notice to act in his stead. We walked up to two houses in one of the big squares, knocked and held up the scivvy and an old fellow at the doors. Up one stairs with half the smart young fellows. Ditto into the next house with the remainder. Into a room on the first floor with Sean and me. Captain Bradford, the court martial bloke, was inside, and he whipped out a revolver and let fly when he saw the pair of us. He missed me by an inch. Him or me, and it was him. There was another fellow in the room sloped under the bed, bawling, screeching, and puking with fright, though he had a gun in his paw. Hemp, begob, the fellow we saw last night. I was going after him when Sean stopped me as cool as you please. 'No hurry,' says Sean. 'Orders are orders. He's not on the list.' So downstairs again, and over two corpses in the hall and women screaming the house down, and away with us and the smart young fellows. Sean sent me to Thomas O'Dea to inquire if he had been raided last night, and sure enough he had been. Auxiliaries, four polite, devil-me-care, hard-faced artists. And nothing else were they in search of but Michael Collins. Thomas took them cool, showed them round, gave them a drink, and bowed them out. I went to Mick and reported. He told me that Sean is to go South tomorrow, and where the Tiger is to meet him."

Condron awoke, heard Dick's news, and sat through a meal in silence, with lack-lustre eyes and knitted brow. Harding looked at a Sunday paper. A line stirred and danced with mad irony under a flamboyant heading: SIR HAMAR GREENWOOD SAYS IRISH SITUATION IS WELL IN HAND. Dick Blake looked up and spoke: "If you were in Mick's place, you would be driven to this. Six of one and half a dozen of the other, ourselves and the British now. Once you start, Heaven alone knows where you will stop, but you keep going. This is the back-wash of the break-down of the truce arranged a month ago. You remember the raids slackened down, and the ambushes, and there was great talk of negotiations. The military party thought our nerve had broken when innocent slobs in the local bodies sent telegrams to Lloyd George." Condron did not speak. The sibyl's books, thought Harding. . . .

The three men strolled down in silence to the match. From groups as they passed they caught rumours of the morning's happenings in excited snatches and lurid guesses.

"Twenty bloody spies. Good enough for them and the dirty work up in the Castle. Torture and murder. Touch of their own medicine will do them good."

"The city will be burned down tonight. It's a crazy notion to go on with the match!"

"Let them get on with their burning, Mr. Long Face!"

"Too thick, all the same, shooting the men in front of their wives! Christ, how would you like it to happen to yourself?"

"Wives? Them fellows has no wives! They done something, you'll find. The lads make no mistakes."

Dense crowds ringed the green field and packed the grand stand. The turnstiles clicked, clicked, clicked as the hundreds and hundreds streamed through the barriers. Harding sighed and looked up at an aeroplane flying low with persistent drone. He was regretting many things: that Captain Bradford was dead, for Papa Shanahan had made him live in lively phrases, the Captain who laughed at the regular death notices which swelled his mail, who sent the I.R.A. to his Majesty's prisons without heat or venom, who thought trial by court martial a fairer tribunal than his Majesty's courts, the Captain who shot first when he went out after midnight to beard Mick's gunmen; that Sean Condron was a marked man; that there were derelicts like Hemp in the world.

Wild cheers drowned his thoughts. Hurlers in black and white were marching down the field to the stirring music of saffron-kilted pipers with beribboned drones aloft and nimble fingers on chanters—a crest of colour and melody on a wave of strength. Play started, and cheers and counter-cheers clashed and echoed and pursued each other and clashed and echoed again and again. A powerful hurler dominated the field, his broad chest spanned with a green sash, his curved and resilient caman driving the swift, singing, glancing ball before him. A hush of warning and dread chilled the echoes of the hurricane of human voices. A rush of feet and a cry: "THE BLACK AND TANS!" A deafening fusillade, and a second. . . . Flashes and savage spitting echoes and wild screaming. . . . The powerful hurler whirled high in the air, his green sash waving, and sprawled flat on his back. A young woman beside Harding fell forward with a sigh, a young man with wiry black hair, who had been cheering, cheering, cheering, sank with a dying groan, clutching his chest, a bloody gash in his forehead. Everywhere spectators were falling, struggling, shrieking. As the second volley died away, Harding, Condron and Dick Blake were carried across the field in the onrush of hundreds to safety. As he went, Harding saw the dead hurler on the ground beneath him, green sash limp and eyes a ghastly glaze. Behind a line of Black and Tans encircled the field. Into the roadways hoardings lurched and burst with a rending crash. On the human wave the three men were carried into lanes and back-streets. They hurried on until they recognised a turning which brought them to Harding's lodgings.

Condron was the first to speak. He looked at the revolver he had left behind him on the bed. He laughed bitterly and slipped it into his pocket, saying: "That wouldn't have done much beyond! But it will later. Did you notice anyone?"

"Hemp!" cried Harding and Dick Blake together.

"Yes!" said Condron. "As the Tans were closing in, waving his gun and howling like a demon."

Again into the darkened streets. Dick Blake left his companions as the lights of the *Emancipator* appeared, protesting that he must go home, as the young one would be anxious. Condron, too, vanished restlessly, telling Harding that he might see him later.

"Terrible times!" cried a jolly constable outside the Central Police Station. "Were you at the match? You look like a ghost."

Harding told the jolly constable briefly what he had seen. The jolly constable shook his head solemnly: "The unfortunate people!" Then he said abruptly: "Kerrigan's within, laying down the law. Come in and I'll take the froth off a pint with you." The jolly constable winked and danced up the front steps, leading Harding past a counter, an inner glass-partitioned room, a passage of cells, down another passage to a large kitchen. A canteen adjoined it, and a hum of talk and glasses clinking and deep voices booming and loud bursts of laughter came through the open door. In the kitchen a constable was chatting to a derelict old man with a shaven head, a red, dirty, withered face and child-like blue eyes. A huge sack was slung over his back. He was gnawing a hunk of bread and gulping now and then from a large mug of cocoa the constable had placed before him.

"I received the Blessed Sacrament this morning. And I met God. God. God and the Blessed Virgin," mumbled the old man. "And I love them both and they are good to me. . . . And the Sacred Heart. . . . And St. Joseph."

"You're real religious, Paddy," said the first constable, immensely edified.

"Not always so!" said the jolly constable. "Nice names you

called me when I woke you up inside the Turkish Bath railings in the Green the other night. There was no mention of St. Joseph then, though you did drag in the Holy Name, and a few unholy ones into the bargain. You're a pretty boyo!"

"Some people is very cruel to a poor old man," mumbled Paddy, finishing the cocoa and slipping the bread into his sack. He shambled down the passage, muttering: "But God is good to me." He crossed himself and vanished.

"A right old ruffian! Cute as a pet fox," said the jolly constable. "As ready to lap up a Protestant bowl of soup or cadge a Protestant pound of tea as any of them from the first proselytising old bitch he meets."

"Oh, Paddy's not so bad," said the first constable. " 'Night, Harding! Gob, yous are a thirsty tribe, you journalists. Michael Kerrigan's within this half-hour, expanding on the day's doings and blathering about politics. And Bolger was within earlier blathering about women. In for your morning bowls on the tick of the clock. Have either of yous a statement to make? I have. I have a mouth on me and a fine capacity!"

They went into the canteen. "My shout!" said the jolly constable. "Three big pints for three sensible men!"

"The Chief wants you, Michael!" shouted Papa Shanahan, striding in with a worried look. "And the subs were asking were you back from the match?" Michael lumbered through the door, breathing vengeance against Milkers and asking the world what was a proper fate for Aristocrats too lazy to find copy placed in readiness on their desks an hour before?

Papa Shanahan asked anxiously: "Where's Bolger? He promised me a black of scenes in the city, and the bloody subs are howling for more copy, though Kerrigan gave them any God's amount to go on with, and I have a cramp in my fist——"

"Another big pint for a sensible man!" cried the jolly constable. "Bolger's in the Fire Station, and he has the black for you all right, but says there's nothing in it. What's your hurry? Sure, Kerrigan will keep them busy within. Begod, he'll make carpets of their guts and whistles of their backbones and give their lights to the crows if they say a cross word to him. Here's health!"

Papa Shanahan brooded, some story seething in his angry, eager eyes. He drained his glass and shoved a second one before the jolly constable, wrinkling his forehead and shaking his head vaguely. The jolly constable told a story.

"Gob!" said the first constable. "I was thrown out of the Ark for telling that one! And that reminds me. . . ." And his

reminder reminded Papa Shanahan and the jolly constable too.
. . . The trio roared in Rabelaisian glee. Then Papa Shanahan
recovered from the mirthful paroxysm which made small rivers
run down his cheeks, and said:

"God forgive us all, and the poor people lying dead in the
field beyond."

"What harm?" said the jolly constable. "We'll be long
enough dead ourselves." But the first constable's face shadowed,
and he slowly shook his head.

Harding came back to the earth with a jolt when Papa Shanahan moved towards the door. The strong beer tasted like water,
and the day's horrors were still bright in his brain. It seemed
to him that the stones of the Police Station were speaking to
him. . . . Here Dan Hogan had lived, moved, and died, and
wave after wave of popular movements had beaten in their ebb
and flow against these walls, and now the latest tide swirled
round yonder tense-eyed groups of G-men, those other simple,
hearty, enormous policemen joking in those great rooms through
which ebbed and flowed, too, the tragedies and freaks, the flot-
sam and jetsam, of Dublin slumdom. . . . "Pups of the same
litter," Bernard Milroy's phrase in the mill, "pups of the same
litter. . . ." And as if to underline the phrase, a young constable
behind murmured: "Bloody work . . . the unfortunate people
. . . sweepings of the jails of England, them and their guinea a
day, the murdering bastards! Wish the Government'd give us
a couple of hundred a piece, and let us clear away to Hell ower
this."

In the Fire Station, Thomas P. Bolger was cross-examining a
cheerful and quizzical fireman on duty, and copying names into
his notebook.

"Sixteen dead in the morgue at Jervis Street Hospital, and
Heaven alone knows how many others wounded in there and
elsewhere," said the fireman. "Terror, desolation, destruction
and bloodshed every hour of the twenty-four. I could almost
tell you the times of the ambushes next week, my hands are so
used to pulling down the switches at the very same hour on that
clock above. And I thought I had left the wars behind me in
France. But tonight I am ready to pull the fire switches down."

Another fireman, merry-eyed, fair-haired and whistling, strode
in, his cap rakish, his red shirt trim and aggressive, and a furnace
in two great blue eyes.

"Dry up, Tom," he cried. "Those artists will get as good as
they give. Mick Collins hasn't lost his wind. Did you see the
bloody Captain anywhere?"

"No, Joe," said Tom. "The old bandjax hasn't shoved his snout in here tonight. I suppose he's snoring above, snug and tight, until the bell goes and the Tans start their didoes,"

And as Joe strolled out, whistling, through Harding's memory flashed and clanged the bells, the red-coated firemen sliding down the long brass poles from their dormitories, bells rattling above the beds, so often restless or vacant now, the swiftly manned engine, the gleaming helmets, the bronze-faced Captain shouting, the horses dashing from their stables in under the harness, the great gates swinging wide, the clang, clang, clang, and the Fire Brigade sailing over the cobbles, any hour, anywhere, with a toss of their helmets, indifferent to oceans of flame, the Black and Tans, riot, war, civil commotion or act of God. . . . Horses? . . . It might be the new roaring motor fire engine too. . . . Swishing hoses, axes crashing, and the bronze-faced Captain booming. . . .

Away then, leaving Tom with ear alert and hand ready to sound the fire-bell. But silence wrapped the terror-clad city, and Sean Condron slumbered on in the little Drumcondra room as calm and still as the sixteen stiff and silent men in King George's Military Hospital, as the sixteen corpses in Jervis Street Morgue—Sean Condron slumbered on, a revolver beneath his pillow. At dawn he rose to speed southwards with the Tiger. . . .

Again the machines hummed and sang beneath Harding's feet and Sean Condron and Captain Bradford and the hurler with the green sash flickered between him and the copy on his desk. . . . Ever faster the machines whirled and whirled and the clock's hands raced onwards. Papa Shanahan was still the link with the outer world, blowing the clouds of smoke from his pipe and planting his voluminous copy before the Chief with eloquent explanation and unpublishable verbal addenda.

Two months after Bloody Sunday, some sixty nights of whirling presses singing an epic of iron and agony, Papa Shanahan's neat handwriting flashed beneath Harding's eyes: "Exhaustive inquiries in the locality by a representative of the *Emancipator* have brought no new facts to light regarding the young man found shot in County Cork yesterday. It has been ascertained that the dead man's name was Frederick William Hemp, formerly a medical student. He was discharged from the Army through wounds received during some of the greatest battles of the Great War. He returned to his native city, Dublin, where he was highly popular with a large circle. Friends and acquaintances pay a high tribute to his brilliant scholastic career, his social gifts, winning personality, and unite in mourning his loss. A total abstainer and non-smoker, he was not connected with any political organisation. The outrage is much deplored locally, and in conversation with our representative, the Rev. Father O'Callaghan, P.P., strongly denounced the shooting, and expressed his firm conviction that no one in his parish had hand, act or part in the deplorable occurrence—the motives and details of which remain shrouded in the deepest mystery."

Papa Shanahan's private version was more explicit:

"Hemp was too crude in his methods. Too many questions about the flying columns in the hills around. Questions to every Tom, Dick and Harry in the local pub, after Mass, on the roads. One night a dark fellow with a scowl and a gun in his fist walked in and out of Hemp's lodgings, and between those two movements, Hemp was no more. He was a spy all right. Those I.R.A. lads make no mistake."

"A great story, Shanahan!" cried Thomas O'Kane, reaching for a telegraph form. "Sit down and write it up. You damned reporters are too damned lackadaisical. Write it up at once." He pinned a telegraph pass to a pile of copy, handed it to a pale youth, and shouted: "Hurry back! I'll be sending down another story to the Post Office at once."

"Take your time, boy," said Papa Shanahan, grinning wickedly. Then, turning to O'Kane, he hissed: "Enough is as good as a feast, Mr. Thomas-Eye-to-the-Main-Chance-Bloody-O'Kane! Write up that story for the *Timbuctoo Gazette* yourself if you're tired of life and a whole skin! But my advice to you is to put up your little book of passes, and get on with your sub-editing and not earn a tombstone before your time. For the *Emancipator* wants no visits from Mick's young men after dark or sledgehammers in the machines. And if they do call, they'll have no hesitation in visiting the consequences on the proper parties. Or perhaps you'd like your ribs roasted after a little jaunt to the Castle in a Tan lorry, like your pal the sub on the *Liberator* they thought had handed in a manifesto from Michael Collins. In this country, just now, freedom of the Press is literally a bloody joke."

Papa Shanahan swept out and slammed the door dramatically. Thomas O'Kane's pendulum eyes swung back to his copy, and he laughed nervously. Between Harding and his pile of telegrams and flimsies and proofs rose the grim dark scowl of the Tiger Doyle . . . "waving his gun and shouting like a demon. . . ." Scarlet as a child caught stealing jam. . . . "Brilliant personality . . . mourn loss. . . . Cat and mouse. . . ."

"Know anything about this fellow, Harding?" asked the Chief, handing down a wad of Michael Kerrigan's copy.

He read: "Arrest of Sean Condron in County Dublin——"

CHAPTER XII

A YOUNG MAN handed a parcel in to Harding with Michael Collins's compliments. . . . Would he visit Sean Condron in Mountjoy Jail and deliver the parcel? . . . The sad-eyed warder casually searched the parcel. Sean talked cheerfully through the barrier. "Thanks for the cake, the handkerchief and the cigarettes. I'll take care to make good use of them." Sean waved a farewell as the sad-eyed warder jingled the keys and droned: "Time up." Good use . . . sometimes Mick's methods were old ones . . . the cake . . . the handkerchief . . . the cigarettes. Through the wicket, relieved to find after a week of silence and gloomy visits from Dick Blake that Sean was detained as a suspect with some vague charge hanging over him. . . . Death sentences were in the air. They would fall when the results of the court martials on the men charged after Bloody Sunday had been promulgated. The Castle net was sweeping wider, and the internment camps were filling. A weary-eyed officer with a typewritten list had called at an old lodgings in Sandymount and inquired for "D. Harding, formerly resided here, deported 1916." Then the weary-eyed officer had worried no more or discovered that Harding was a knight of the pen, and respected the liberties of the Press. But the officer's visit gave Harding an added thrill when lorries with glaring headlights stopped outside his door. And thousands of Dublin citizens had the same quick heart-beat too after Curfew and a not unfriendly feeling when the revolvers of the gunmen cracked at too-zealous G-men and the secret agent of the Castle. For private spites were active, and the military raiders sometimes said that there were very bad neighbours writing in on the quiet to pay off old grudges and enliven respectable localities with raiding parties. . . .

Back to the machines and headings, to the markets reports, the ambush report and a St. Vincent de Paul report with the names of all the drapers in Dublin many columns long.

"Don't cut those names," said the Chief. "Space for the Pillars of Charity, Church and the *Emancipator*." It was a joke against him. In the days of his inexperience he had thrown a column of such names at a similar gathering into the waste-paper basket; he and the Chief had spent a frantic quarter of an hour in salvage on the eve of Press. It was an even worse nightmare than when he had nearly fined the wrong milkman, saved only by the Chief's eagle eye and mine of a memory. The Chief was a fighter. Not in vain had he fought for the Greeks in his youth, sniping the Turk and scouting along hillsides for weeks at a time; and with a bang of his fist on the table said he was ready for any bully at any time, from Advertising Managers down. . . .

A telephone bell rang. Papa Shanahan rushed in. The Chief sat up. A sub-editor shouted the news from an agency flimsy. The one story all: SEAN CONDRON ESCAPES FROM MOUNTJOY JAIL.

The cake . . . the handkerchief . . . the cigarettes . . . key, file, invisible ink and tobacco smoke as a smoke screen to it all. . . . Mick's old dodges . . . and Sean could climb any wall . . . the lads outside with a rope, descent, escape. . . . It had all happened before, as the street ballad ran:

> *Some forty Sinn Feiners, like acrobat trainers,*
> *Skipped over the high walls, alive, alive, O!*

Home through the darkened streets. . . . Sean Condron was asleep within. . . . A clock in the distance boomed: four. A lorry rattled outside, and stopped before the door. . . . A powerful searchlight was flashing from an armoured car in the rear. . . . Sean Condron slipped beside Harding into the front room. . . . Had the weary-eyed officer changed his mind? . . . Condron smiled. Above the engine's din a woman's shrill voice rose derisively:

> *O Hurlers, Scholars, Saints and Bards!*
> *Says the Grand Old Dame Britannia,*
> *Come along and enlist in the Irish Guards,*
> *Says the Grand Old Dame Britannia,*
> *Each man who treads on a German's feet*
> *Will get a present of a parcel tied up neat*
> *Of a tombstone cross and a winding sheet,*
> *Says the Grand Old Dame Britannia!*

Lorry and armoured car slowly crept from view with blinding white flails of light across roofs as they went. . . . The singer's mocking voice died away. . . . The conscientious officer who gave everyone a Curfew lift was on duty. . . . Condron would not discuss the escape. . . . Oh, a file, a rope, a wall. . . . Mick's message? . . . Oh, something on tomorrow. . . . To sleep then.

Despite Harding's arguments, Condron went casually down the steps next morning. Before he left, he asked: "Heard about Tom Hughes? Since he was wounded in the Bloody Sunday shootings, he has been in the military hospital. He was court martialled last week. We hear he's next on the Castle hangman's list. There's not much hope for him or the three condemned already. But Mick doesn't quite agree."

Michael Kerrigan's wad of copy explained the hard and meaning gleam in Condron's eyes:

"One of the most exciting incidents among the many which crowd fast one upon the heels of the other during the present time occurred shortly after noon today. From eyewitnesses an *Emancipator* representative learned that a party of young men entered the Military Hospital and went straight to the ward where Mr. Thomas Hughes (whose death sentence was promulgated this morning) has been lying since his court martial. Prior to the arrival of the raiding party, Mr. Hughes had been removed under strong military escort to Mountjoy Jail, and the guard of detectives and military in constant attendance in the ward withdrawn. Finding their quarry flown, the raiders hurriedly decamped. Subsequently there was considerable military activity in the vicinity, several city residences were searched, but no arrests were made. Inquiries in official quarters failed to elicit confirmation or denial of the report that a rumour of the projected rescue had come to the ears of the authorities. Mr. Hughes, a poet of some distinction and popular with a wide circle in the capital, was deported after the 1916 Rising."

Amid the masses of proofs, a week later, Harding caught sight of a heading: MOUNTJOY EXECUTIONS TODAY. ALL HOPE GONE. He went into the Reporters' Room and looked at the assignment book: Mountjoy 4.30. The machines whirled and throbbed below. His work was over, but he could not rest. He went downstairs and watched the white cascades of newspapers falling from the singing presses and being hurried in bundles from the dispatch rooms to the waiting vans. Into a van with himself and Michael Kerrigan and towards Mountjoy while it was still dark.

A small crowd watched the windows of the prison. Once and then again lights showed and died away. Tom Hughes ... Nineteen Sixteen. ... Poet. ... All Hope Gone. ... The sky was brightening slowly. Vague khaki groups with bayonet and rifle patrolled the roadside; aloof, dumb, detached spectres. The crowd grew. Candles were lighted and a murmur of prayers deepened. The guards at the entrance and the armoured car prepared to move and the crowds closed in nearer to the barred gates. . . . Harding saw Michael Collins beside him. Mick was watching the distant windows. A woman's sob was heard. . . . Morning flooded the sky. Over the kneeling people a great sigh passed. A whisper: "They are gone!"

The armoured car wheeled and drove away. The soldiers marched off, faces impassive. The iron gates swung open. Fierce-eyed young men and kneeling women changed into a restless and leaping wave plashing against the main iron gates of the prison. A wicket opened. A warder posted a white paper on the gate. The fierce-eyed young men tore it down. A woman swooned with a cry of agony. "Tommy's wife!" . . . the words came across to Harding. . . . The crowds melted to half a dozen fierce-eyed young men. But when Harding left, Michael Collins was still there, gazing at the windows, tears in his eyes. . . . Thinking of Tom Hughes. . . . Thinking hard and bitterly.

Again the clock's hands racing and the humming below. . . . Scenes and casual phrases of Easter, Nineteen Sixteen, dancing and peeping. . . . Tom Hughes and words from his poems and a great chorus from the whirling machines: IT MIGHT HAVE BEEN YOU. . . . Not David Harding, but Thomas Hughes, Tom Hughes, a pale face and shotgun against the window he guarded and the desolate street outside and the circle of flame and BOOM, BOOM, BOOM, a puzzled man with a shotgun worrying over his poems against war in Jim Larkin's *Worker*. . . . Jingling phrases . . . borrowed phrases, but he loved them. . . . Leaves in the wind. . . . In his grave, soon thicker with dust than his poems in the pages of Jim Larkin's *Worker*. . . . IT MIGHT——

Above that chorus from the machines and the chaos of his thoughts rattled the sound of rifle-fire and revolver shots and the bursting moan of grenades exploding. . . . A machine-gun tap-tap-tapped almost outside the *Emancipator's* walls. . . . Lorries and tenders rumbled over the cobble-stones. . . . Again the zip-zip of rifles and the moans of explosions and a scattered series of revolver shots and the machine-gun tap-tapping. . . . A telephone bell rang behind Harding, and Papa Shanahan's voice sounded in his ear: "Yes, Shanahan speaking—that you, Harding?—the bloody night-town reporter must be over in the police canteen or down in the kips, begod, but for God's sake take the message. A street battle near Westland Row. Ambush outside the station. Four Volunteers dead. Three Auxiliaries, too, and several wounded. I.R.A. ruse. 'Phone message to Dublin Castle earlier that seditious meeting was in progress in hall in vicinity sequel to execution of Hughes, no doubt, but don't write that or the Chief will have a fit. Three arrests, including Edward Malone, elderly man, Co. Dublin, former deportee, that's all, and give the wire to the night-town fellow to follow up, for I'm off now."

Again the telephone: "Military G.H.Q. speaking. Would you take down this little communiqué? Are you ready? 'At nine this evening Auxiliary Cadets and military raided Emerald Hall near Westland Row Railway Station. Bombs were thrown and a number of revolver shots fired as the Auxiliary Cadets approached. The fire was returned, and the attackers fled in disorder, leaving three dead and a quantity of arms behind. Three arrests were made, including one man found to be in possession of an automatic revolver. There were no military casualties.' That is all. Thank you. Good night."

A tired and passionless voice died courteously away. . . . The door opened, and Michael Kerrigan appeared, gloriously drunk. "I'm off today, boys," he shouted, skipping hilariously to the head of the table, and planking a wad of copy before the Chief. "But I love me country, every blade of grass, and I love the *Emancipator*, and here's an account of the ambush. I walked through it. A bullet tore the tip of my boot. I asked a policeman what was up, and he said, I declare to Jesus, he said, yes, he said, the thick ejot he said: 'Mr. Kerrigan, I think there's shooting going on somewhere.' Shooting! There was, by the seven snotty-nosed orphans, there was! And they've taken old Edward Malone, and they'll hang the unfortunate man, for there are three Auxiliaries dead. . . . And here's the best copy in Dublin from our own war correspondent on the spot, but not on duty, though always loyal to the *Emancipator*, a better national newspaper than the rotten *Liberator*, the nagging factionist foe of the Party, weren't the people of this country brought up on the *Emancipator* and the *Key of Heaven*? As long as we remember, weren't they brought up, yes, a better paper than any paper on the face of the earth in spite of all the milkers, alleged gentlemen, and dud sub-editors sitting on their backsides round this table here before me? Ye can play yere golf and laugh while the old ship drifts on the rocks and batten on the long-suffering reporter. Oh, ye bloody thieves! But Michael Kerrigan, who doesn't have to look up any place outside the suburbs of Dublin in a sixpenny geography, will never let the *Emancipator* be stuck, though others reap the reward of his blood and toil. So good night, Chief, and to bloody Hell with the Government, for when the Government starts hanging, Michael Kerrigan, still loyal to the Party, has no arguments for the young fellows." And he skipped out lilting: "Oh, all around me hat, I wear a tricolour ribbon O!"

"Head him off, Harding," said the Chief, blandly scrutinising the copy. "Good stuff here. Get more facts from him. He'll walk in to the Editor if you don't grab him quick. All journalists in that condition do. It is a law of nature."

But Michael had vanished into the night of Curfew. The jolly constable on duty eased Harding's mind when he rang up the Police Station at the urging of the alarmed sub-editors, who had forgiven Michael his invective and quailed at his possible fate.

"Mr. Kerrigan is safe in his own domicile," said the jolly constable. "Constable 215B has just reported his safe arrival there, to the joy of his lawful and long-suffering spouse. The constable who encountered Mr. Kerrigan on the way thither, singing the 'Soldier's Song' and calling for cheers for Charles Stewart Parnell and discoursing, accompanied him, fearing that his eloquence might annoy the Curfew patrols, and you can't take any chances with those little gets—— What's that you say? We'd be as bad! We would not! Let them say a word to us and we'd give them a welt of a baton as quick as we'd look at them, and if their superiors demurred we'd just sit down on our fat backsides and do nothing for them—and well they know it! Anyway, several patrols encountered happily failed to comprehend the gist of Mr. Kerrigan's remarks. The presence of Constable 215B and his assurance that Mr. Kerrigan was legitimately abroad and possessed the required pass smoothed all obstacles. You fellows have grand times! The Press for ever! Good night!"

Then as the machines whirled louder, Tom Hughes faded from Harding's memory and Malone . . . Malone . . . and Bernard arguing with him came back . . . the same Malone . . . "a crack at Carson" . . . Bernard glaring . . . the mill . . . poles pounding like the machines. . . .

Throb, throb, throb, thump, thump, thump . . . the machines whirled . . . one night . . . a streamer across the page . . . MOUNT-JOY EXECUTION . . . MALONE HANGED . . . the machines whirled . . . the clock's hands raced . . . on and on. . . .

Clang, clang, clang . . . the red-coated firemen were dashing away to the blazing Custom House across the river. . . . And the *Emancipator* shook to noise of the battle between Sean Condron within and the Auxiliaries without . . . the flames reddened the skies, lapping, leaping, roaring. . . . Dick Blake and his men had lowered their revolvers and walked out of the Fire Station only two minutes before . . . but the fire fighters were too late then . . . the flames danced with a song of doom around and far above the green bronze dome. . . . Sean Condron limped past the *Emancipator* office, one of the few who had escaped to life and freedom from that howling furnace of the Custom House. . . . Michael Collins watched from his quayside window, and deplored in uncompromising terms the secret 'phone message which had interrupted his well-planned attack . . . the Auxiliaries drove past beneath with their dead and prisoners. . . .

But inside the *Emancipator* the machines sang the epic of a nation, singing, throbbing, humming, clanking, thumping, on, on, on. . . . Custom House in ruins . . . ten thousand pounds on Michael Collins's head . . . two ambushes a day in Dublin . . . raids, arrests, dead men in fields, babes born dead in the stress of it all . . . blood at noon . . . death at midnight. . . . Machines whirling, throbbing, humming, singing a nation's epic. . . . ON . . . ON . . . ON!

CHAPTER XIII

ARTHUR MACKEN sighed and a fatigued expression came into his keen eyes while he awaited the return of the Tiger from Dublin that fine July morning in the small farmhouse. For seven months he had been "on the run" in the South of Ireland, if to lead a flying column, aided by the Tiger Doyle and Terence O'Donovan, is to be "on the run." That morning, as he waited, he asked himself, in the tone of one who expects no answer to his question: "I wonder if this life will ever end?"

Mick had recalled Terence O'Donovan to Dublin, and then the Tiger Doyle. The bright-eyed little Volunteer was even now guiding the flying column deeper into the hills. Dispatches had been captured which revealed the secret of the small farmhouse only a week ago, and Macken's secret and Terence O'Donovan's secret too. But the farmhouse remained unraided, and Macken regretted yielding to the bright-eyed little Volunteer. No word had come from the Tiger or Mick since the short message the day before the dispatches had been captured: "Tiger Doyle returning tomorrow week." No answer to his report of the capture. So Macken blinked in the early sunlight, seven months' terror and counter-terror shaping themselves into one colourful, endless, aching phantasmagoria.

Only the day before yesterday, he had lain hidden for six

hours in a house, and military lorries panting outside with head-lights a-glare. A swarm of trench-helmeted searchers in khaki foraged the houses on either side and opposite his hiding-place. Macken had watched within, finger on revolver trigger, agog for the raiders who never came. False starts, one knock on the door, the search-lights playing a moonlight dance through the front windows, a weary voice shouting commands to the troops to retire—and then sleep from very exhaustion. Even now the engine of a military lorry drew nearer and nearer on the main road, troops singing loudly. A whiff of petrol, fainter singing, silence again. . . .

Implacable blood-lust and terrible tools of war! Romantic Tells and Hofers and De Wets in the history books, elusive Spaniards and fleeting Mazzinians, perhaps they too knew the Tiger Doyle, snarling at his men, a revolver in each hand, oaths spitting between his set teeth, dark eyes aflame: "Fire at the belly and then at the head, and if that doesn't finish the bastards, empty the rest of your guns into them." The Tiger Doyle, last to retreat of fifty active, striking, fleeting, fighting men defying all the Black and Tans and troops in a single county. . . . The Tiger Doyle, Arthur Macken's striking arm.

Striking arm. . . . Murders on one side, executions on your own. . . . What's in a name? . . . He recalled giving an order to the Tiger Doyle and two worried-looking men, an order which had not cost him a wink of sleep. . . . Six shots, a labelled and riddled figure lying in a ditch. "Spies and traitors beware." No, not a wink of sleep. . . . One of his own young men shot in the jail beyond in Cork City after the weary legal farce to save his life in the courts. And when they had shot him, some said that the officer in charge of the firing party had turned away, calmly filling and lighting his pipe. . . . Not a wink either. . . . It didn't do to be too sensitive. Michael Collins and the small band behind the guerrilla war hadn't much sentiment either. . . . As little sentiment as their foes. . . . Blow for blow. . . .

Macken looked out impatiently. It was full morning, and Curfew had lifted in the great city some miles away. The peace of the quiet countryside through the windows lulled him. The captured dispatch and the tarrying Tiger nibbled behind his ease, and his thoughts turned to the labelled and riddled figure in the ditch again. Spies they were everywhere, from the masked spotter glaring through the windows of a jail exercise yard to the quiet commercial traveller in the hotel lounge. And getting near to the flying columns now. Wish he could lay his hands on that prowler who had called at their old headquarters in the little village beyond, Saturday fortnight, and asked for him and the lads by name. Knew a lot, that fellow—clever and courageous, and more subtle than Frederick William Hemp. Stayed a night and vanished into space. Good woman of the house had warned them when he had called again, placed a light in the kitchen windows as directed when he had retired, but the fellow had vanished five minutes before the Tiger Doyle had dashed up the stairs. They had scoured the countryside—hills and roads and bypaths, but the man must have known the district like a map. "Good luck to him," Mick had said. "Too smart for you sleepy louts."

No place like the South when it came to terror and counterterror. Executions in the morning and shootings and ambushes in the evenings. Lorries bristling with guns and steel, and all the tension and devilry of war abroad throughout the countryside. That lorry in the streets of Cork, three days ago, one man stone-dead beside the driver, and four others leaning against the sides with glazed eyes, bloody faces and chests. Two hours afterwards, armoured cars and a fleet of tenders dashing through Patrick Street on a mission of retribution. The village and town nearest the ambush had blazed that night. There, beyond all places in Ireland, Macken felt the psychology of war, and the stand of a whole population against overwhelming force. "If we only hold out," the young man murmured, "nothing on God's earth can beat us." Very quiet they looked, these young men, who struck and ran and frayed their enemies' nerves to pieces with seven devils of pride and obstinacy in them. And at the back of them a nation with seven devils, too, throwing a glamour over all the horrors of self-defensive vengeance. And deep down in Macken's heart, compassion and pride and weariness wrestled.

"No weakness, Danton!" the phrase flashed in and out of the colourful, aching, endless phantasmagoria of Macken's thoughts, back from the long ago when books were mightier than arms, back to the night when Mick, in argument with O'Donovan, had upheld the Quakers stoutly, and Terence O'Donovan had laughingly quoted the phrase, and Mick had argued obstinately ahead even while he sent the Tiger on a more congenial errand. Then Mick had banged the table and said a Quaker world would be a better world, an old fellow in the train a week before had told him so, and there was no answering such men. And Terence O'Donovan, shrugging his shoulders, had said he hoped that he would be dead long before either of them lived in such a cabbage-garden planet as the Quakers wanted. And the Tiger Doyle, packing his revolver into his pocket, had said that he had read Tolstoy on Harding's advice, and his own honest opinion of that old cod was that he was like half the old fellows in the sodalities of Dublin, an old ruffian, who had had his whack of war and women and wanted no one else to have his bit of fun.

Macken paced the floor impatiently, and another picture came into his mind. And a phrase. "To those who endure the most. . . ." Greatest words uttered in all that dark nightmare of war which shook his very soul in quiet hours like this. War, bestial school of experience at best, which stirred up the darkest instincts of man. Even war for Ireland. . . . It was not all war though. . . .

"To those who endure the most, not to those who inflict the most suffering—VICTORY. . . ." Away in Cork Jail there had been a most obstinate miracle of a struggle, keeping time to the tragedy of Brixton Jail, where Terence MacSwiney with those words on his lips had wasted to a defiant shade. His death had shaken the world. Cork Jail. . . . Macken, in disguise, had entered and seen the eleven young men himself.

For ninety-four days the eleven men had fasted and withered behind the thick grey walls. A group of relatives, Volunteers, Cumann na mBan sympathisers, maintained a constant vigil. As a wicket opened, there was a glimpse of sand-bags and sentries within. Each evening large crowds gathered with hymns and prayers. A poignant and peaceful scene, amidst the foliage, the rushing stream and the trams on the Western Road. "No perceptible change," said the newspapers towards the end.

"No perceptible change" meant this. Relatives and visitors would tell you—hadn't he seen it himself, and didn't the memory haunt him?—that the prisoners were slowly becoming skeletons, breathing with difficulty and semi-conscious for the greater part of the twenty-four hours. The wind stirring through the cell windows and the silent corridors outside was more audible than the breath of the dying men. Warders and sisters glided noiselessly past. Watchers kept a constant and terrible vigil. The men lay prostrate the whole day long, rallying at times, smoking, laughing, wondering how long the ordeal would last. And through ninety-four weary days the shadow of Death crept nearer.

In the prison, Macken had smelt the ever-present odour of Death. In white-washed cells on trestle-beds lay eleven men whose marble-lined faces betrayed little beyond the white and tightened skins, but their corpses were bloodless and shrunk appallingly. Two died, and it was said you could lift their dead bodies like a feather. MacSwiney died, and still the struggle wore on. . . .

Outside people had discussed hunger-strikes. Some said it was overdone, and but an appeal for mercy, an attempt to lacerate your enemy's heart instead of breaking his head— quoting John O'Leary, implacable bard-like old Fenian in whose grave Yeats had buried romantic Ireland years before—John O'Leary who would never do anything that admitted his foes were not barbarians. Others said that so spiritual a protest was a better foundation for the Republic than policemen's bones. Different opinions were voiced. It would never do to give in. The men were done, anyway. Better let them have the glory of it. Still, after all, said the bright-eyed little Volunteer, still after all, Life was sweet! Then the Dublin message which ended the lingering agony: as they were prepared to die for Ireland, let them be prepared to live for her.

Macken sighed, smoking cigarette after cigarette. Michael Collins had nearly brought a truce nine months ago on the eve of Bloody Sunday. . . . Well, what did it matter, anyway? Fight it out now and spare the coming generation. Stop once, never start again. Unless this Terror was broken, what life was worth living? He looked back over nights of danger and days of weariness and pain, the deaths of men he had grown to love, the grim routine of ambush, attack, pursuit, and knew he would not blot them from his life if he had the choice. . . .

A lorry swept in under the front windows and every pane trembled. The door beneath collapsed with a splintering crash, footsteps thundered on the stairs, and through the windows he saw a line of khaki and trench-helmeted men and blue-uniformed, white-faced Auxiliaries closing in a circle around the small farmhouse.

·   ·   ·   ·   ·   ·

Macken sprang to his feet, but too late. The door swung open, and rifles covered him. He saw more khaki and trench-helmeted files on the landing. Sounds of search came from below. Auxiliaries with revolvers drawn strode from room to room shouting. Empty all, with the column among the hills. Nothing for the raiders, not even the Ford with patched tyres, not a gun, a bullet, or a compromising note or piece of writing in Arthur Macken's pocket.

Looking with a curious impersonal excitement at the revolver muzzles now pointed at him, Macken handed his notebooks and correspondence to the officer in charge. An Auxiliary glared at Macken and yelled:

"You bloody I.R.A. assassin!"

How like the Tiger Doyle! Except that the Tiger was polite to prisoners, even when he regarded their funerals as imminent. . . . In level tones Macken told the officer a well-prepared tale: John Duffy, electrician, 15 Frederick's Row, Rathgar, Dublin, on holiday in Tim Warren's farmhouse in absence of Warren on business in Dublin. He hoped the officer would not detain him until the Dublin addresses were confirmed or notice the six-months-old dates on the letters when Thomas Warren had sold the property finally to Mick's agents. . . . Wait till Tibb's Eve, the day after the Day of Judgment. Searchers below re-reported: nothing found. "Go back and look again!" An Auxiliary, small, sandy-haired, keen-eyed, came in and asked politely by sheer force of habit:

"When did you see Michael Collins last?"

The officer in charge frowned sarcastically, and remarked very loudly that this was County Cork, not Dublin. Macken again repeated his well-rehearsed tale: John Duffy, 15 Frederick's Row, Rathgar, Dublin, staying in Thomas Warren's farmhouse in absence of Warren in Dublin. Never saw Michael Collins in his life. Didn't know one end of a gun from another, and didn't want to. Hadn't been in the Great War, as he had to look after his widowed mother at 15 Frederick's Row, Rathgar, Dublin. Old friend of the Warren family. Only interested in electrician's work. The small sandy-haired Auxiliary and the officer consulted, the Auxiliary wrinkling his brow in abstraction and stealing side-glances at Macken from time to time. Macken caught the officer's words: yes, though the information in the captured dispatch had seemed promising, what had they found to confirm it? Better be on the safe side, fellow's story consistent enough, didn't answer O'Donovan's description, *Dublin accent*: Terence O'Donovan's English as Michael Collins's Cork. Another mare's-nest. You had to be careful with private spite and leg-pulling and lists of good loyalists' houses sent to provoke raids by the funny Irish. Better let him go. What had they found? The sandy-haired Auxiliary reluctantly nodded agreement, but still knit his brow over Macken's correspondence which the officer impatiently handed to him.

"What's this?"

The excited Auxiliary who resembled the Tiger Doyle knelt on the floor and glared at the boarding. New nails. Wrench, wrench, wrench, tappings on the walls, revolvers again levelled at Macken's head. Five well-oiled rifles beneath the flooring, a cloud of plaster from the walls, but nothing in the hollow spaces. A flood of abusive questions from the glaring Auxiliary. Macken, knowing the game was up, still obstinately harping on John Duffy, 15 Frederick's Row, Dublin, no connection with illegal organisations, gunmen everywhere, house vacant some time after Warren went to Dublin. Officer muttering these damned gunmen would fool anyone, they were so glib and looked so innocent. A shout from outside: ammunition in the outhouse under the floor. And grenades. And two shotguns. Macken, still level and voluble, looks quietly at the glaring and raving Auxiliary's revolver as it taps on his right and left cheek-bones.

The small sandy-haired Auxiliary looks up quickly and smiles! "You are cool enough to be one of the boys, and you are a liar! I remember now. I have raided Frederick's Row in Dublin. Only ten houses. No Number Fifteen."

With an inexpressible look of blended fury and amusement, the officer orders Macken under arrest. . . . A reek of petrol, a loud explosion, and the gutted farmhouse broke into flames. . . .

Along the winding roads towards the barracks, tenders and lorries humming and jolting, a glimpse of the Tiger Doyle and the bright-eyed little Volunteer lounging against a wall. ` . . Too late. . . . Death in the barrack square soon with an officer lighting his pipe. . . . Should he dash for it and cheat them? . . . The Auxiliaries look away with cat-and-mouse looks in their eyes. Too obviously careless looks. . . . "Shot while trying to escape." No thanks. . . . Hopeless unless the Tiger——

The lorries roll through the barrack gates, and past barbed wire, sand-bags and gleaming bayonets within. Macken is conscious of the sandy-haired Auxiliary and a masked figure peering through the guardroom window. The masked figure bows its head and steals away. . . . A Spotter. . . . A lot of trouble. . . . They must know him. . . . Auxiliaries enter. . . . Hard-eyed Auxiliaries, but nonchalant. . . . Questions, questions, questions . . . his description read out, old Dublin report, Dan Hogan's hand in every line, the evil that men do lives after them, the good, etc. . . . know nothing of his seven months in the South. . . . Bloody Sunday shootings . . . wrong there. . . . But only defers the agony. . . . "Closely in touch with Michael Collins." . . . Why hadn't they noticed the initials on the dispatches: A.M.?

A train shrieking and swaying towards Dublin. Six Auxiliaries on guard in the carriage, hands on the revolvers strapped to their thighs. The small sandy-haired Auxiliary in a corner smiling to himself. Arthur Macken is nearly as good a catch as Michael Collins. The train shrieks into a wayside station. The glaring Auxiliary who so resembles the Tiger Doyle gulps feverishly from an uplifted whiskey bottle. But Macken is enacting a familiar farce beside him: the court martial at this journey's end. Yes, polite officers, bored somewhat, draughty rooms, long formal documents, a courteous President, trembling civilian witnesses, if any. Refusal to recognise the court. Perhaps Mick would forbid that and send a learned counsel to harangue the court. Else: "Citizen, oh, no, you are a soldier of the Irish Republic and refuse to plead. Plea of Not Guilty entered." Judge-Advocate weighing the evidence. Court closes to consider its verdict. Officers re-enter, more polite and bored than ever. Bad sign that. "Decision will be promulgated later." That's how the farce would go. Bloody Sunday on the brain. A rope or bullet, anyway, when the seven months in the South came out. And the farmhouse arsenal in martial-law area. Rope or bullet? That was the choice. . . . Only one end now. . . . A run for his money. . . . Do it again. . . . Why didn't the train start? The Auxiliaries stirred uneasily. Tiger Doyle's double gulped a final draught from his bottle and passed it to his neighbour. The sandy-haired Auxiliary studied Macken's face with a sly and gloating satisfaction.

"PUT THEM UP, YOU BLOODY WHORES!"

The Tiger Doyle was glaring into the carriage, a revolver in each hand, oaths spitting from his lips, his eyes rolling in his dark face, and three armed men behind him. The small sandy-haired Auxiliary's hand flashed to his thigh. Macken clutched the throat of the glaring Auxiliary in an iron grip and seized his revolver. The small sandy-haired Auxiliary and a companion sprawled writhing on the floor to the roar of the Tiger's revolvers. Macken and the Tiger's double staggered into the corridor and on to the platform. The little bright-eyed Volunteer was courteously detaining the grinning fireman and driver beside the engine. A small group of Volunteers were on guard outside the station. Macken's head struck the platform heavily. He wrenched the revolver free and fired. A cry, a stinging pain in his shoulder, and he sank into darkness to the roaring of the Tiger's revolvers and the wild shrieks of the Auxiliaries. . . .

CHAPTER XIV

ARTHUR MACKEN opened his eyes with an intolerable ache in his head and shoulders and the colourful, endless, aching

114

phantasmagoria of his life in the South recommenced. He looked around. Michael Collins was seated at the bedside, poring over a mass of papers and smiling to himself. The bright summer-evening light flooded the room. Children's voices playing floated in from the street. Dublin accents. An Angelus bell. Six.

Mick spoke: "A narrow shave, Arthur. But you are all right now. The wild times will be over soon." Mick turned away brooding. Back into Macken's mind rang the Tiger's revolvers and the grey stealing into the shocked face of the glaring Auxiliary after Macken had fired. Collins completed the tale. Three Auxiliaries dead, three trussed up and left on the platform of the wayside station. The Tiger Doyle had driven Macken to Dublin, where he had lain delirious for the best part of a week. Soon be round again, doctor said.

Macken knew where he was when Winifred Considine came in. I.R.A. nursing-home on the outskirts of Dublin. He sank to sleep and Mick went out softly. He opened his eyes again and the room was dark except for a flickering night-light. The colourful, aching, endless phantasmagoria began again with sharp stabs in his head and shoulders, and Collins's words singing in his ears: "The wild times will be over soon." No, they would go on for ever. Mick was mad. The Tiger Doyle would never stop shooting until his brother rose from the dead, and that would be on Tibb's Eve, the day after the Day of Judgement. Unless this Terror were broken, what life was worth while? England would never agree to Dominion status unless the Republic were round the corner. Deadlock, trial of two wills. Handful fighting, hunger-striking, speech-making, shooting, "on the run," in and out of jail. Neither could give way. A word would do it. What word? Glaring Auxiliary just now, only really wanted to drink whiskey, and good stuff he had chosen too. Smelt good. Someone's darling. Sorry he's dead, and I killed him. Well, why didn't he drink his whiskey and leave me alone? Only yesterday outside Frongoch, . . . back in Dublin while the eternal Great War dragged along. Not so sorry for the little sandy-haired fox the Tiger laid out. Knew too much, that fellow. At the guardroom windows with the masked spotter. Too good a memory. . . . No Number 15 Frederick's Row, Rathgar. Only ten houses. Smiling in the carriage corner. Quiet ones always the worst. Quiet enough after the Tiger Doyle. . . . "Bloody whores!" . . . So they were, but why did the Tiger only swear when he was shooting? Clean-spoken man otherwise. And told his men to swear and spray with verbal sewage the human targets they shot at? To work themselves up. Cuchulainn's charioteer, Laeg, did the same at the Fight at the Ford when Ferdia was winning. Books long ago. Yes, Laeg said to Cuchulainn: "Alas, indeed, the warrior who is against thee casts thee away as a trollop would cast her love-child! He pierces thee as the felling axe would pierce the oak. He darts on thee as the hawk darts on the small birds, and thou hast no claim to valour or bravery until the end of time, thou little fairy phantom." And Cuchulainn cast the Gae Bolg, the thirty-barbed spear, through Ferdia, his friend, over whom he wept, "and a trance and a faint and a weakness fell on Cuchulainn." Propaganda old and new. Laeg and Tiger Doyle. Arthur Macken and the glaring Auxiliary. Tommies raiding and I.R.A. gunmen plugging, all swearing virtuous saints, calling on Heaven with Hell in their hearts.

Great War had finished and Little War had followed. . . . Peace Conference futile hope. . . . How Germany had crumpled. . . . But Ireland hadn't. . . . Clash of two wills would go on for ever and ever. . . .

Clash of two wills. . . . Whole people facing the Conscription crisis with tense and frigid will, ready to die in the nearest ditch with pitchfork and shotgun. . . . What about his tobacconist gyrating around the spirals of moral and physical force, genial huckster who sold Union Jacks on Armistice Day as a profitable sideline and tricolours the weeks before and after? . . . First declaring for the last ditch, and that England should have her bellyful of fight, and then three days after with equal emphasis that passive resistance would prevail against gas shells. . . . Wobblers, wobblers all. . . . The mass was always like that, up in the clouds one minute, down in the gutters the next, but mainly intent on four square meals a day and the sins of their neighbours. That was why Mick kept them at fever heat. . . . Clash of two wills. . . . But Mick said the wild times would be over soon. . . . Mick was mad. . . . Dictator. . . . Dragon's teeth.

Phantasmagoria colourful, aching, endless with the night-light's circle on the ceiling. . . . That waitress in a Dublin café, in and out of every ructions since Nineteen Sixteen, telling her mother she had come through once and would again, and if she didn't it couldn't be helped. . . . That gruff Dublin working man with seven children at home, who had sprawled, a riddled corpse, in the Harcourt Street ambush. . . . That bloodthirsty slum-bird Halpin who went out to bomb lorries every night he was let. . . . The mass of the people with set teeth behind Michael Collins. . . . Clash of two wills. . . . As hard as the

English now . . . hard, hard. . . . Perhaps they would go. . . .

Why should one sacrifice the people for a phrase? . . . How long could it last? For ever and ever. Sharp twinges shot through Macken's head and shoulders. . . . A gasping cry escaped him.

Winifred Considine came out of the shadows and handed him a glass with a dark liquid inside. Macken sat up and saw the summer light through the darkened curtains. The life of the great city sounded afar off. Away, far away, too, shots sounded faintly and the roar of lorries. Clash of two wills for ever and ever. . . . Macken drank the liquid and sank back into his drugged sleep with the colourful, aching, endless phantasmagoria growing fainter and fainter. Ten struck, and with the Curfew hour the life of the great city became mute and a deadly quiet fell with twilight on the streets.

.   .   .   .   .   .

Michael Collins had glanced at his watch ten minutes before while he looked down on a quiet Dublin square from the top window of the third house in a side-street which adjoined the square. . . . He listened to the distant ambush in the falling twilight. . . . The Tiger Doyle entered, and then Considine and Sean Condron.

"Another ambush," said Mick. "Mighty near Curfew. Ten to ten. Nine o'clock Curfew tomorrow, I suppose—or perhaps not."

His eyes twinkled quizzically, and then a gust of anger turned his face into a scowling and angry mask.

"Orders are orders!" he growled. "I sent out word yesterday that the ambushes were to be slowed down——"

Considine broke in:

"The order was questioned in Sean's company, and, anyway, we couldn't get in touch with the active service men——"

The door opened and Terence O'Donovan came in, unusually grim. He looked at Mick angrily, and said sharply:

"Dick Blake came to me for confirmation. He couldn't find you anywhere, since your time seems to be taken up with politicians lately. I am responsible for tonight's ambush. I told him to carry on, pending further word from you. The order came into force only tonight, and I thought the instructions yesterday operated from tomorrow night. Dick Blake wants permission to decoy the Auxiliaries from the Castle——"

"Tell him he won't get it!" said Mick. "Change in policy. The citizens are grumbling, and I don't blame them. We haven't scored but one hit in all the ambushes in the Dublin area. Tonight's a detail. A detail, Terence. You were always a stickler. No reflection at all. Your British Army training has left its mark. We poor louts can't work to timetable."

Terence O'Donovan frowned impatiently and asked for news of Macken: "Leakage of information, the rifles, grenades, ammunition and the farmhouse gone!" he cried reproachfully. "Why have you kept me here these past months cooling my heels? The men are leaderless——"

"Not at all," said Mick soothingly. "Since the Little War has started, every active service man is a natural leader. We have rescued Arthur Macken. We have not lost one man of your company. You trained them so well, Terence, that they go like clockwork. There's something more important to discuss. I have called you here tonight to tell you——"

Ten struck outside.

Lorries with wheeling searchlights rumbled past below. The powerful lights played on the windows, and then stabbed the darkening thoroughfares, north, south, east and west.

Mick glanced at some papers he drew from his breast pocket, and studied them closely.

"They'll just miss us," he said. "Let them have their last fling."

More and more lorries roared into the street, and the sky blazed with searchlights. The Tiger Doyle crept to the window, opened it noiselessly and looked out. He turned, and his face was pale and his eyes danced with excitement.

Twenty yards away from the little street troops were jumping from the lorries and closing the adjacent square with barbed-wire entanglements and stout barriers. Searchlights were crossing and recrossing the roofs and windows. Search parties were hammering loudly on the doors. Shouts and wood splintering. The inhabitants were being hurried into the street, and lined up on the pavements.

'It's a mixed raid," whispered the Tiger as the others joined him. "Military and Tans." Mick smiled and then sighed as angry questions floated up:

"Where is Michael Collins? Don't tell us your damned lies! We know everything. We know he's hiding here!"

"You're foolhardy, Mick," muttered Considine. "When you knew the raid was coming, why didn't you change the meeting-place?"

"No time," said Mick. "Besides these copies of their orders I hold in my hand show they'll only raid the square. They'll just miss us, I tell you." Then he said, as if thinking aloud: "What an irony if they blundered into taking us tonight!"

Suddenly a searchlight veered from the roofs of the square, played down the dark street and shone full on the watching face of the Tiger.

"Put your bloody head in!" shrieked a thick and angry voice. A shot followed, and the sound of a bullet striking the ceiling of the room. Light flooded the street, and the Black and Tans dashed in, hammering wildly on the doors. Soon the familiar chorus reached the listeners:

"Where is Michael Collins? None of your damned lies! We know he's hiding here!"

"The garden's clear, Mick!" snarled the Tiger. "Let you hide there. Leave the rest to me!" His eyes shone with a fierce and exultant light as he dashed down the stairs. Entering a lower room, he calmly watched the raiders through the window curtains. Mick and his companions had gained the small garden and scaled the walls, vanishing into the darkness. All save Sean Condron, who joined the Tiger.

"Clear off to Hell!" he snapped. "This is my job. I've been chasing that big Auxiliary, whose voice I'd know a mile away, for twelve months, and I'm going to get him tonight for sure!" The Tiger covered a huge Auxiliary through the window, whispering: "There he is, the bastard! I'll redden the pavement with his lights before this night is much older."

The big Auxiliary was brandishing a revolver in the faces of a group in night attire shivering on the pavement. He howled monotonously: "Where is Michael Collins? Shot my only brother, he did! Wait till I meet him! Wait till I meet him, the dirty murderer!"

"Mother of God!" gasped the Tiger, dropping his revolver. Michael Collins came calmly down the steps of a neighbouring house, chatting in high spirits to the raiders.

An Auxiliary was questioning him and laughing at his replies.

"This is a respectable street," Mick was protesting. "Look at my papers. I am a clerk in the Castle. We have no sympathy with rebels in this locality. Do we look murderers? It is distressing when those we look to for protection treat us like the Sinn Fein riff-raff would if they had the chance. I shall write to the *Irish Times* about it."

An angry British officer was remonstrating with the Auxiliaries:

"This street was not to be raided. Collins was hiding in the square. And has escaped by now, thanks to your foolery. Don't make damned asses of yourselves! The residents here are loyalists. There will be the devil to pay."

Some yards away a plain-clothes detective watched the scene. A look, almost a wink, passed between him and Mick. The Auxiliaries went back to the square, shouting a farewell: "Keep away from the —— windows!"

Mick rejoined the small group in the garden. "Couldn't resist that empty house," he chuckled. "Belongs to a Castle official who's on holidays. I was afraid the Tiger would shoot the big fellow, and I can't afford to lose the Tiger or to have sensations in this respectable funk-hole."

Then he added: "Our shooting days are nearly over, lads. Within a week the British will agree to a truce." Considine and Terence O'Donovan turned sharply towards Michael Collins. And in quick and eager sentences, and with a light in his grey-blue eyes, Mick began to speak.

CHAPTER XV

THE Truce came, a suspension of the abnormal, a fevered Truce in which horror and death grew dim. Curfew lifted, and for the first time in many months, the Dubliners could walk the streets until morning if they wished. The children burst out from the slum coops and celebrated the fall of the barriers with bonfires, which flickered in back-lanes at first and spread hourly over the main streets. Tricolours waved in tiny hands over the blaze, fed too often with hoardings, old furniture or tenement banisters. Tiny voices chanted popular ditties. Begrubbed and barefooted, the children played with masks and pistols on the city bridges or trekked on wooden box and wheels over the dusty tram sets towards the wonders of the Dublin hills, singing, trudging, fighting, shouting to the blue, green and gold, to pine trees, bracken, endless slopes, demesnes, pools, ruins and back again, singing, to the slum coops.

Half the adult population watched the comings and goings at the Mansion House, swarming before the friendly sanded crescent beneath its two stately storeys to debate the ethical cut, thrust and parry of the London negotiations and cheer Michael Collins as he swept up the steps, stouter and more genial since he had come "off the run." Here and there on the quaysides, in O'Connell Street, at Kelly's Corner, at Leonard's Corner, or even beyond Portobello Bridge on the Rathmines Road, a revelling citizen pirouetted and collapsed in an eloquent whirligig on the pavement, to the censorious grins of the steadier citizens and the discreet backs of the police.

Forests of tricolours surged up in the thirty-two counties of Ireland. Many estimable citizens betook themselves to martial ways, training in I.R.A. camps, and loud in praise of guns and gunmen, but perspiring under the intensive training and discipline of those same gunmen with the hard glances and bellicose voices. Young men trooped out from the wired-in wastes of the internment camps with madness in their eyes. The flying columns marched down from the mountains to blazing bonfires and wild welcoming shouts in the villages. The machines in the *Emancipator* sang a normal tale at last, tale of a convalescence overshadowed by a threat of further surgery.

A darker and darker shadow crept into the eyes of Thomas O'Dea, the eyes which could read Dublin with the experience of forty years spent in the shade of the Custom House. Arthur Macken limped in to see him and to cheer him with the facetious judgement:

"We have seen the last of war. Both sides are too cowardly to start again."

"Let ye keep that way," said Thomas, glowering. "Time for ye both. Nothing but letters, letters, letters every time the word 'Republic' is mentioned, a hitch, and off ye go again dancing round each others' corns. And at home we have all the old cods of both sexes who'd have fainted to hear a slap-bang during the Terror howling for blood like blazes, and hanging out the Green, White and Orange. The country grows madder every day with drink and nerves and tall talk. I wish it was all over one way or another." But Arthur Macken shrugged his shoulders, and Dublin went on amusing itself or waited in greater and greater crowds outside the Mansion House.

A foreboding note crept into the singing machines of the *Emancipator*. Throughout the South the Truce continued with some minor hitches between the I.R.A. liaison officers and the British authorities. But one night that Harding remembered for ever, the Truce collapsed in the North. The great machines shrieked a sudden song of doom, and Belfast shaped itself in his memory, from the telephone, with Papa Shanahan speaking in his ear, to the warning outlines of Papa Shanahan's copy before him and the story Edward MacTaggart shouted aloud from a flimsy. The fury and desolation of one night's rioting had deepened into a street battle, with the I.R.A. sweeping the Orange quarter with a machine-gun and snipers on the roofs.

The British military authorities, deaf to the Falls Road and Sandy Row tom-toms, awoke to the crisis and sought the liaison officers of the I.R.A. Castle officials rushed northwards to preserve the shaking Truce.

Belfast seethed in Harding's mind: fierce eyes and harsh accents, shawled mill girls, a line of police closing the connecting streets between the two hostile quarters, children digging up "kidney pavers," bottles hurtling in the air, cries for the Pope and cries against him, stones wielded in well-swung stockings, women in hushed houses anon covering up corpses with white sheets and praying and cursing fervently as the age-old tide of death ebbed and flowed in up-to-date Belfast, the stalwart Northerners scorning to run from peeler, Papist or Williamite, glorying in the ancient boast even now uttered by Edward MacTaggart: "When a Dublin crowd is thinking of running away, it's then that a Belfast crowd settles down to a nice wee riot, and puts away a trifle for the summer holidays with the loot!"

Edward MacTaggart's eyes were heavy as he jested. Thomas O'Kane snarled, memories in his pendulum eyes, Papa Shanahan's voice droned in Harding's ear again: the rioting had slackened; interviewed the sad women wrapping their dead in shrouds while the conflict died down behind the military cordons; "and as serious as you please, a cousin of the first fellow killed yesterday told me about the Orange casualties tonight: 'bad bastards, the lot. Their last words were, "To Hell with the Pope!"' "

"True till death!" interjected Edward MacTaggart, his eyes twinkling. "That's the spirit we want."

"You're delighted," rasped Thomas O'Kane. "The same black drop in ye all!"

Papa Shanahan's voice again. Details, details, details. Belfast mourning her dead, on a wilderness of kidney pavers, bleak as a Liverpool back-street, as a fog over slums in Southwark, bleak, bleak, bleak. . . . The telephone bell rang off. Edward MacTaggart sadly weighed his headlines and cross-heads. The Chief slashed his blue pencil through O'Kane's summary of the riots, and handed it back: "Less petrol, O'Kane, less petrol!" O'Kane's arms waved and the room watched a miniature riot in his snapping eyes. "Barbarians!" said someone at the lower end of the table, and two Northern accents rose in rugged and furious unison: O'Kane and MacTaggart defending their boyhood's city.

Belfast under Curfew, ticked the racing clock, bleak, bleak, bleak, shots, women huddled behind windows, still forms under white shrouds, death in dockyards, murder in murky lanes, all in the name of Jesus Christ, silent now. Merry sounds came in from the Dublin streets. The Chief passed down another wad of copy and flimsies to Harding. All quiet in Belfast, names of dead and wounded.

One name sprang to life in the flimsy which curled in Harding's shaking hand. A ghost stirred in the Dublin Post Office, on the Connemara hills, at a table in Havensfield. WINIFRED CONSIDINE. Victim of a stray bullet, mortally wounded, died some hours after in hospital, sister of Dermott Considine, Havensfield, Dublin, no doubt of identity of victim or truth of the story. As he pencilled the headlines, Harding felt a stab of horror, not at another death, but horror at the sudden thought that he had lost all capacity for feeling.

Later, beneath the swinging arc lamps in the quiet streets, surged up memories out of the past in the years which had flown, in the times when youth had not been grey. That was poignant; but that was all. A gleam of beauty in the lurid years. A name with its roots in old memories. One gracious life broken on this wheel of revolution. A lessening of the sweetness of the world. A sentiment, what more? He had rarely seen her when she had visited Dublin at intervals. Once, twice, three times in all she had written to him, and her straggling hand always evoked the Five Days and Havensfield and the Connemara bogs and lakes and the moment he had known the Irish Revolution would waken the quietness of those distant hills. Some curious fog invaded his brain, a Belfast murk, a numbing deadness which came between him and all zest of life. Well, what of it, after all?

A thousand similar tragedies had been compressed into five years which history books would never mention or, at best, dismiss in a line: men taken from their beds and shot, struck down on lone hillsides or murdered in fields; women killed by stray or nonchalant bullets; children maddened or smothered in the womb; civilians mangled in the city ambushes; seeds of insanity or consumption sown in the internment camps—epic never to be told, of humble martyrdom already half-forgotten in the lengthening Truce. Aye, what of it, after all?

The dawn, grey and spectre-peopled, surprised him sleepless and with a heartache and weariness as huge as all the vague and unsubstantial shades which lurked in the hours preceding. He thought: "The Revolution is taking everything, our hopes, our dreams, our loves, our humanity. Would Victory console or move us now?"

123

A light broke in his mind even as he asked the question. They had all held out, the whole people, Michael Collins the fighter, Considine the dreamer, Arthur Macken the organiser, Dick Blake and the Tiger Doyle, gunmen, David Harding, observer and provider of news, Winifred and Agnes MacGowan and Dick Blake's little daughter, May, and Thomas O'Dea, fifty sturdy fighting men in every county, and thousands behind them. They had all held out as no generation of Irishmen and Irishwomen before them, when hope had gone and great ships had sailed unregretted to freer worlds. They had all held out with aching hearts and set teeth. For what?

And in December a mocking answer came: PEACE.

CHAPTER XVI

PEACE! In the small hours of a December morning, Edward MacTaggart handed half a sheet of flimsy to Harding. Agreement had been reached, and a treaty signed in London by representatives of Great Britain and Ireland. It was late, and the remaining sub-editors had already put on their hats and coats. Half their number had gone home. All the evening rumour had chased rumour, but now the Chief was wrestling to fit in the unexpected news at the "stone" below, scanning the reversed type, "killing" the least important stories and listening with knit brow and eyes aglow to the yeas and nays of the printing-room foreman. The formes were locked and the presses started to the taps of hammers on the leaden semi-cylinders from the foundry, false starts and then a hum. . . . Wearily, less wearily, the machines sang: peace, Peace, PEACE! A white cataract swirled from the presses to the waiting vans. PEACE! The *Emancipator* posters shrieked on the building's front . . . one word . . . five deep black letters. PEACE!

"Well?" asked Edward MacTaggart. "What do you think of the news?"

Harding found the simple question a hard one to answer. He could only think there were five letters in the word and it sounded well. No emotion stirred within. He looked at the faint print on the flimsy, at the fresh copies of the *Emancipator* someone threw down on the table, at the poster the Chief pinned on the wall for a profound and merry scrutiny. Peace, an anti-climax to the rumours which had chased rumours, one wilder and more melodramatic than the other, but six, four, two hours before, and the Chief shaking his head despondently as doubt and tension deepened. An anti-climax, too, after the meeting with Terence O'Donovan earlier that evening in a café.

Considine had brooded in silence at the table. O'Donovan had spoken with a bitter candour:

"Peace? There will be no Peace. It's breaking-point. They have orders not to sign if allegiance or partition is pressed. Breaking-point! We are as far apart as the poles. We stand on the Republic. They on the Empire. We should never have gone to London."

A gleam of anger, and he went on:

"Michael Collins wants peace at any price. He always courted the limelight. He wants a safer and bigger stage. He picked the negotiators. He would have taken the terms of a year ago, the terms of July last. His hand has been everywhere restraining, and where he could, corrupting the militants. Before the Truce was signed, he stopped the city ambushes. He has kept me here in spite of every protest. He is nothing but a crafty political intriguer and dictator rolled into one. He's gone soft with self-indulgence and rotten with swelled head."

"But he works!" said Harding angrily. "He found a wilderness of talkers and a country drifting to chaos, and he ran a revolution on business lines. He answered letters and found arms and money, and broke up the Castle Secret Service, and used every weapon that came to his hand. He knew his mind long before you did, and if he abandons the Republic now, it may be because he knows Ireland better than you do, lost in your rigid little self-admiration cliques! Don't talk to me of intrigue and self-indulgence. He's lived with his life in his hand for years, and if he can take a glass with the boys when he has nothing better to do, he knows when to stop. He hasn't smoked since he went "on the run." He tells all the vain little humbugs he meets the truth about themselves—that's the cause of the host of little gnats ready to slander him and salve their wounded vanity. You ought to be ashamed to make such charges. You remind me of a Castle Red Hat writing his reminiscences! And there's excuse for the Red Hat. Mick never kept the rules they made. He gave them blow for blow and lie for lie——"

Considine laughed and nodded his head:

"You are a pragmatist, Harding, and a hero-worshipper to boot. Michael Collins did all you say, and he was right. What gave him the right to act at all? The Republic! Which exists. Otherwise we should have taken Home Rule——"

"You would have if you had had the chance," said Harding.

"Don't wave phrases at me. The country would have pelted us with bricks, even after Nineteen Sixteen, if we hadn't taken it——"

"True," said Considine. "I know your arguments, and there is truth in them, as far as the facts are concerned. There is also principle. The majority was never so advanced as the small minority our history proves is always right. Listen to me: today we have one hope of a lasting peace, not the stepping-stone to our ideal, not practical politics, not counsels of fear, but an honest formula which acknowledges Irish independence first, but gives England all the military safeguards she requires——"

"I see some work for politicians there!" said Harding slyly.

"And you are right," said Terence O'Donovan, frowning. "God help us if we start swopping formulae with British politicians. Dominion Home Rule is better than all this new juggling with constitutions based on Cuba and the United States's association with the Allies in the war. For Dominion Home Rule might not in the end bribe and hold Ireland, but your new association would be too much for the British politicians to give and too subtle for the Irish mind. No, independence. We began. Let us go on."

As they argued a fog of unreality rose between Harding and the two men opposite. Words, he thought, and the real opinion of Ireland that the *Emancipator* presses seemed louder than these precise and angry doctrines. Words, still words. . . . Why didn't Terence visit pubs sometimes? He said as much.

"Your profession prejudices you, David!" laughed O'Donovan. "And you have gone from bad to worse. From one vendor of drugs to another. But talk as you will. In ten years you will give a very different reply to the question: 'Who was the greater, Pearse in Nineteen Sixteen or Michael Collins now?'"

Six struck, and Harding had risen to go. Considine's words had floated after him: "Demoralisation . . . war weariness . . . the place-hunters gathering like vultures . . . psychological effect of the Truce . . . they will split Ireland. . . ."

In the street Dick Blake strolled, whistling. He was going to the mill. Sean was above, as mad on drills and freak mobilisations as ever, doing Napoleon and sweating the lives and souls out of the post-Truce recruits, lads with no honest pride at all to come in the day after the fair in the first case, and to put up with the insults they got in the second.

"Are you pessimistic, David?" continued Dick. "Meaning, of course, are your hopes of a settlement extra weak? Grand word, settlement. Mick says the fellows in London will sign.

I hope so, bejaney, for one shell or one angry bullet would send these new post-Truce buckos helter-skelter back to their funk-holes. Gob, you should hear Sean telling them off. Small credit he gives them for joining in after the racket stopped, and he rubs it in how glad they'd be to see the barbed wire of an internment camp when the trouble begins again. Hard to blame him when you hear the windy britches praising the old gun and not believing Sean telling them that there's a big drop in store for them. And for yourself and myself into the bargain, David. The bloody military will mop up the poor old *Emancipator* next time as sure as God made little apples, for they hate you newspaper fellows turning the light on their little games, and as for me, oh, I was never born to be buried in Glasnevin. So long now."

Peace? What wonder that Harding shrugged his shoulders at the meagre announcement and Edward MacTaggart's question and walked home only half-believing that a miracle at the London conference had stilled the last ripple of the stone thrown in Nineteen Sixteen, and calmed the five years' agony. In the morning the stupefied and wondering Dubliners were talking without committing themselves. Better wait and learn what it all meant. Too often had peace balloons soared, to crash flaming to the ground. Concentrated times had blunted the edge of all surprise.

Yet business men and traders rejoiced at the news. By noon the citizens drew a deep breath and smiled:

"True enough. The news is in the bloody papers all right!"

"Thank God it is all over!" said the Lord Mayor of Dublin at a charitable meeting in the Dublin Mansion House, outside which half the adult population still lingered. Murmurs rose from the crowds watching there. Rumour, rumour, rumour.

"A near thing! Arthur Griffith pulled his tie straight, a real danger signal that, as everyone will admit that knows him, and made for the exit, all his papers tight under his oxter, and, bejaney, the beans would have been spilt, only Lloyd George raced between him and the door, and planted his back against it, saying: 'Mr. Griffith, as one bloody Celt to another, I implore you——' "

"Thirty years the old Party was talking. Look at what these lads have done in five!"

"The gun did it! Nothing like the old gun!"

"Fat lot of shooting some people done and blowing out of them now! Yous told that to the Tans, didn't yous?"

But another shadow fell over the cheerful crowds even while

127

they scanned the Treaty terms in the next morning's *Emancipator* and *Liberator,* and rolled the many legal phrases and eighteen clauses aloud. A subtle unrest emerged from the Mansion House and spread through the city. Terence O'Donovan came out, and then Considine, silent and sombre-eyed. They walked ahead, unheeded and unheeding.

"Irish Free State. . . . Oath of Allegiance . . . share of public debt. . . . Irish military force. . . . Provisional Government," droned the eager crowds. Michael Collins passed in, his dark hair a plume of triumph, his grey-blue eyes alive with fun and purpose, his jaw set, up the steps in one bound and wild cheers around him. Again the murmurs: "Northern Ireland . . . constitutional status . . . common citizenship . . . British Commonwealth of Nations . . . Irish Free State. . . ."

"But it's not a Republic, and there's a split within."

"It's a grand settlement, whatever you say. The substance though not the shadow."

"I tell you, Mr. Know-all, there's more shadow about it than substance, and you will still have to get the British Government's permission to build a lighthouse. In black and white they have laid that down! Is that the freedom we strove for? Eh?"

"Ah, go away ower that! You and your bloody lighthouse! Some fellows is always looking for bloody trouble half-way."

"Tell that to me elbow!"

Through the city went the wind of doubt and speculation. Dick Blake looked up in his simple back room from a study of the *Liberator* and the evening papers which briefly announced the division of the Mansion House leaders.

"What's come over them all?" asked Dick. "I'm fed up to the teeth with these didoes! If it's good enough for Mick, what's wrong with it? Can't they do the one thing, anyway—take it or leave it?"

"Lloyd George has wiped their eyes! Commend me to a Welshman!" cried his little daughter, May. "I never trusted that fellow an inch."

"Devil a wipe! What's wrong with the Treaty? An Irish Army, an Irish flag, Customs and Excise, Ulster in unless she votes herself out, an oath God Almighty Himself couldn't make head or tail of to George Rex, the immediate evacuation of the British troops, and England nailed to the bargain in the eyes of the world. What more do you want, child? We'll get the rest in time."

"I am surprised at you," retorted May with spirit. "We want

128

a Republic. That Treaty has a catch in it somewhere. The old cat there could tell you that much."

"The old cat," chuckled Dick, "is like the rest of Ireland. He wants a quiet time and four square meals a day. I know what's at the back of all your old gosther. Them wild young ones of the Cumann na mBan would demand the surrender of the British Fleet if our men had come back with a Republic. Aye, begod, they would so!"

"None of your jeering!" cried May, a dagger in each eye. "Foolish girls in skirts are better than old women in pants any day of the week. You must be getting old. You were a better man when you laid out the bobbies in the big strike in Nineteen Thirteen, and fought for Ireland in Nineteen Sixteen, and helped to send the Tans to Kingdom Come since. I never thought I'd live to see Lloyd George wipe Mick's eye and my own father's eye."

"Lloyd George will live in history for that, anyway," said Dick, rising. "And now so long; I'm off to have a pint. No respect for parents nowadays."

Thomas O'Dea looked up sharply when Dick asked a leading question:

"I want to forget the whole damned nightmare. Do Considine and O'Donovan know Ireland? Mick does. They might if they worked behind this counter three nights a week for ten years. We are the hardest-headed race in the world, for all our poetry and idealism. Mick is the real martyr in this crisis. He's sacrificing his reputation to save the faces of British and Irish politicians. A good bargain if the British clear out and leave us alone. Let them call it what they like if they only go."

"You are too hard on Considine," parried Dick. "The Republic still exists, and Considine——"

Thomas frowned and laughed:

"Dick Blake, outside Considine's brain, the Republic only meant independence, and the secret Republic we backed for five years died when the men went to London. We were caught in a cleft stick, and we may as well admit it. Forty years I've worked behind this bar, and I know a fact when I see it, and a man when I meet one. I've seen Mick at work, and for all his faults he's the greatest man in Ireland. He smashed the Castle with its own weapons, and if there were four million Michael Collinses in Ireland we should have the Republic—or four million Considines either. But Mick used the crowd who never understood Considine's dream."

Dick Blake looked morosely in front of him, five years' memories teeming in his brain:

"A big climb down, all the same, Thomas. And the crowd cheers the dream, anyway. The thought gnaws at me that Considine and O'Donovan may be right. All our old enemies are against them. And we are signing under duress, too."

Thomas laughed:

"A big climb down? All life is that from childhood to the grave. But say a halt half-way up. We all change. The wars have blown the bottom out of everything. Duress, you say? England is signing under duress, too, and wait till you hear the grand names she'll call the process!"

"The young lads who died——" began Dick Blake, but Thomas broke in:

"There's a limit to tears of sympathy, and all this bone-rattling will harden the heart of Ireland. Europe is too full of graves with dead men and weeping women. If the Nineteen Sixteen dead and the dead of the Little War came to life, they would argue the case on its merits and not think they were as infallible as the Pope because they did what every young lad in half the countries of the world did in the Great War!"

"You are right there," said Dick, "and a bloody pity any of them had to! Fat lot of good wars bring to the working man. Another pint and have one with me. When our own Generals are ten years older—and Sean Condron in particular—I declare to God we'll have to pension them off or plug the lot. And the lads 'on the run' will be the new aristocracy, hob-nobbing with this new Governor-General bloke mentioned in the Treaty; a serious source of weakness that. Trust them to find a soft job for all their broken-winded Dukes and poor but blue-blooded relations. Begod, I'm a Bolshie from this out!"

But Thomas O'Dea declared that he would argue no more. He only wanted to see an Irish flag over Dublin Castle before he died, and all the old cods in Rathmines and the Kildare Street Club as purple as turkey cocks with rage, and all the pot-bellied inspectors saluting Michael Collins in his new uniform.

Brightening at such a vision, Thomas O'Dea moved on to his work, humming a street ballad:

> *Seven hundred years, seven hundred years,*
> *A foreign flag had flown,*
> *Had flown so long e'en Irishmen*
> *Thought it never would come down.*

But one bright Easter morning
Our eyes beheld with pride
Green and White and Orange
Float o'er the Liffeyside.

Dick Blake turned out along the quays and crossed O'Connell Bridge. He sauntered on towards the Four Courts, with its emerald curve in the distance against the evening sky. A pity all that had gone in the wars. Great work for the builders when all was fixed up! That young one at home teaching her own father, oh, giving his sense for a child, well, let her go to blazes her own way, she was near seventeen now. Black and Tans. Always stood up to them. Including the time a revolver was clapped to his head in his own home at midnight, mercy of God they didn't look under the floor or they'd have found something that time. "Do you believe in an Irish Republic?" says a big fellow, an ugly customer with dyspeptic cod's eyes and his liver rotten with whiskey and a sandy moustache bristling over his crooked teeth, and one leg as stout and as stiff as a cannon. The lado the Tiger Doyle could never meet. "I do," says I, "and what's more, if you're going to shoot me, do it quick!" And the young one bawling the house down for all her old talk now. And the hard nail went off laughing enough to split himself, and saying he'd a better use for good bullets and grinning out of him: "You're a cool one!" And the lads in the mill said that Dick had no right to act the hard chaw and give out his old guff to a dangerous mad ruffian the like of that. Well, his nibs was gone back now to sing hymns in the village choir and blow about taming the wild Irish and share out the loot with his pals and keep chickens, the bitch's bastard. And Mick had sent the Tiger special orders to behave himself the night the fellow caught the boat with the rest of his dirty companions.

The Tiger Doyle and Sean Condron stepped from the shadow of the Four Courts.

"Good night, Dick," cried Sean. "Have you joined the Imperialists? Did you hear the city companies are refusing to give up their arms and the Army will have a word to say about this betrayal?"

And away citywards went Dick and Sean in eager argument, the Tiger Doyle striding along beside them without a word.

. . . .

Harding scanned his book-shelves while he waited for Macken. He was glad that a free evening intervened during the long debate

131

in the Dail and he would not have to scan the long columns of speeches for another night. His fingers wandered aimlessly to a small yellow-covered book in dusty condition. Years since he had opened it. *Bodach An Chota Lachtna*. Churl of the Drab Coat! The title evoked the past and his dream of Michael Collins. Not such a bad shot! That picture of Ireland's agony which had obsessed him for five years seemed strangely unimportant. The old dream took on new shapes in his fancy. Fionn and his warriors hooting the Bodach. Considine and O'Donovan sniping Mick in the Dail, in little papers, on every city hoarding and tram pole. The dream died and his reflections were tinged with bitterness. Every road he had travelled had ended in a dead wall. His pacifism was a personal mood, a reaction from Easter Week. His writing was lost and dusty already in the files of the *Emancipator*. And when he had fought in Nineteen Sixteen, and when he had remained at the *Emancipator* desk, it had all been one. A bright morning ending in a grey evening. Politician, gunman, merchant, monk, ordinary citizen, it was all the same in the end.

Below this mood a serener wisdom glowed suddenly. A feeling of oneness with the agony of a people endured to fulfil the hope of the centuries. An epic was ending with waving banners and warriors feasting. Soon the music of harpers and the songs of poets again. Hope blossomed. . . . The tricolour was on Dublin Castle, and the old Ireland, foredoomed to defeat and futility, seemed gone. They belonged to the time of revolution. Their best days were before them, and they could build a new Athens on the Liffeyside, an Athens worthy of the hills and sea which framed the fairest of cities. Hope was stirring in Dublin, a capital again, such hope as had not stirred for a century or more. What mattered if the individual life was broken and heart-ache ended all personal dreams? And looking back in that intense moment, he felt that he had lived only in the Five Days and in the years he listened to the song of the presses and watched Dublin in her agony from his sentinel tower. Here were the roots of his life and such wisdom as he had found. . . . The ground was cleared for the builders and all the murk and evil in the old Ireland was passing. . . . There was a step on the stairs. Macken entered, whistling. His visits had been more frequent since the Truce, although he spent his days in drilling young men and disappearing down the country on periodic trips. He was thoughtful, and a hard light shone in his eyes. A whimsical expression passed over his face, more pallid and meagre than usual. He sighed:

"The Dail debate has adjourned again. Every deputy of them all must speak to posterity at appalling length. They know they'll never get the chance again. Talk, talk, and talk everlasting. Shouldn't be surprised if the Treaty goes overboard. Mick is telling the world in the lobbies that it may be defeated by a few votes——"

"Does he believe that?" asked Harding sourly.

"He believes it's safer to scare the wobblers who want safety and glory," said Macken smiling. "Don't you know Mick's tricks by this? I don't blame him. Here I am, an auditor of the debate, exhausted. The strain was terrible. Nothing but ghosts and realities wrestling in clouds of words. Then the knowledge that such and such a deputy has got up with a different opinion every morning. And darker knowledge than that. The danger of a general explosion before summer, for the Tiger and his friends have broken loose. Do you know that the Dail was guarded by Mick's orders yesterday? Wild country Commandants were dreaming of a *coup d'état*, if the voting——"

Harding was impressed by Macken's intensity. Arthur Macken was no alarmist, and his words chilled Harding's roseate hopes of an hour before. Intuition and experience told him that Macken spoke the truth, but he put the knowledge aside as quickly as he could, and wrapped his self-deception in words of encouragement:

"The Dail will ratify. What's got on your nerves are your country Commandants with swelled heads. Don't mind them. If they hadn't gone over the line, all out, they wouldn't have got as far as they have. That was their job. No one dared to teach them to think during a revolution, and much good it would have done them if anyone could have. Why shouldn't they cling to their dream Republic? Hasn't it been drilled into them for the past five years?"

"Yes, reason is out of it!" admitted Macken.

"Then there's human vanity. People are arguing: Michael Collins is a great man. A Republic is greater than a Free State. We are Republicans. Therefore we are greater than Michael Collins. They state a case."

Macken shook his head:

"Oh, change the subject. There's only one bright thing about it all. This opposition may do Mick good and keep his head the proper size. West Cork democracy will begin to ask otherwise, and Dublin the day after: 'Yerrah, who is this fellow, Mick Collins, anyway? Don't we know him well? To Hell with him!' "

133

"Tonight we must go a-visiting," said Harding. "Let's drop over to Agnes MacGowan."

But if they changed their place they did not change the subject. Tobacco smoke and controversy clouded the atmosphere of Agnes MacGowan's flat. Patrick Edward MacGowan alone was silent, an aloof and charitable pipe a-smoking as of old. Michael Collins was arguing in a corner with the Tiger Doyle, who was vehement and explosive. Agnes moved vivaciously from chatting group to group.

"Isn't it sweet that peace has come?" she was saying. "No, of course, it's not all we could hope for, but then, all those poor young men died to free Ireland and not for explicit understandings and details about ports and customs and all that."

Macken's eyes roamed to Agnes's book-cases, and a window beyond. Guns behind the cases, Michael Collins sliding to safety down the slates and Hogan balked again, Dan now as dead as mutton. . . . Dangerous vigils since she had watched the Easter fires. . . . Spitting venom at the midnight raiders, Auxiliaries, khaki, all one. . . . Women, tigers in wartime . . . purring now, claws sheathed . . . too good to last.

He looked round. Considine, with troubled eyes, listened to Sean Condron, talking, talking, talking. Sean's voice rattled and rasped. Damn him, could he find nothing else to talk about? "No use trying to fool England." Hold out for what you wanted. He had fought for his Republic, who the devil asked him, and he would have his Republic. Treaty good, very good, too good, no stepping-stones for him, bread of the existing Republic, what did the oath mean?

"God knows!" said Considine. "I don't. Political egg-and-spoon race. Mick should know better than that." Then Considine relapsed into silence and refused to argue; as Condron continued to rattle and rasp, he rose suddenly and walked from the room with glowing eyes and the eternal spectre of his Easter failure goading him on from behind.

Michael Collins finished his argument and came across to Macken. His eyes were merry when he spoke:

"The Tiger and company mean business. Good hearts and fiery heads. I know the mad plans they have afoot: bank raids and breaking the Truce and nobbling the Army. But I'll talk them round——"

"No, you won't!" said Macken fiercely, a savage bitterness in his tone. "Talk to them straight and tell them you won't have any damned nonsense, and tell the country their plans. Fight them now or quit! And don't try either soft-soap or underground intrigue. A war party always wins with time and secrecy on its side. Don't *you* know that?"

"I would rather go back to the guerilla war than that!" said Michael Collins, striding out, vital and confident.

Macken mused on human capacity to believe what it wanted to believe. Here was Michael Collins gambling on human reasonableness, he usually so clear-headed. No, the revolutionary tide would submerge him ere it ebbed. Ireland was behind him, because Ireland knew instinctively that he was her bulwark against chaos. But she would break him as she had always broken her greatest. A chill swept over Macken as in one clear moment he sensed the truth and the days and things to be endured to the end.

Nodding curtly, Terence O'Donovan came through the door. Some people loved war! Ought to know the devils he was calling up from Hell. Lost in the mists after he had found himself in the wars. Didn't know the slime and dirt that would be stirred up in the next six months. Why, it was starting now. Mick's turn and then yours, Terence! The wind of Revolution was blowing through the room. It sounded in the shrill voices and forced bursts of laughter, gusts of fable and slander, a chronicle of fantasy and personal bitterness.

Voices, voices, voices: "Back from London with gold in their pockets." . . . "Lloyd George's whiskey must have been extra good." . . . "Collins was never in an ambush . . . always a bully, takes oaths with the left hand." . . . "Why didn't they shoot the fellows who signed the Treaty when they stepped off the boat?" . . . "Oh, give them a chance, lads! They'll have the Republic in a hundred years, and jobs for themselves in the meantime."

Macken plunged into an argument with Terence O'Donovan and six others. He joked and chaffed, but his antagonists' solemn humourless faces froze him to the soul.

"How can there be Civil War?" asked Terence O'Donovan. "Maintain the existing Republic. If England won't go another inch and declares war, that is her lookout. We are only saying what you said yourself for the past five years. You led ambushes. You shot and killed. You sent men to their death. What alone gave you authority? The Republic!"

"Yes, when you were fighting for European freedom, Christianity, Democracy, small nations and the rest of it, and keeping your full-blooded oath to the British monarch," said Macken calmly. "Yes, before you agreed to negotiate to have your cake and eat it. But when the Treaty was signed, the situation changed at once."

"A possible and honourable position," said Terence O'Donovan courteously, and fell silent. A lively voice rose in the distance, an eager voice whining nasally:

> Oh, we'll to the Treaty stick,
> Sure it's good enough for Mick
> And the Father and the Mother of Sinn Fein.

The words drawled and twanged in Harding's ear. What did these fevered controversialists know or care about the people of Ireland? These mild philosophers, word spinners, scheming, jealous mortals, gunmen, women, doctrinaires and that songster yonder? A fat lot he sang to the Black and Tans. "Where's the bloody cat?" said the mouse. Ought to have his tonsils seen to, the thick ejot! The *Emancipator's* presses droned another song in his ears, the murmurs in Thomas O'Dea's shop, the mild young man, victim of the city ambush shrieking curses and his foot shattered, casual remarks of policemen, firemen, the real opinion blown in unpublished whispers across the desks of the *Emancipator*. . . . "Good enough for Mick. . . ." Oh, forty more verses, and his only handkerchief is in the wash. . . .

Before Harding's mental eye the faults and virtues of Michael Collins filed and passed. Let them yap! There was a man. Knock him out of the picture, and where was their movement? Back to the debating rooms, a thing of words. . . . "The wind and the sun flamed . . . ."

Agnes MacGowan swooped: "And why are you moping apart when all the fun is beginning?"

"Fun?" asked Harding as he thanked her. "What of yourself, with all these martial chimes and funeral chimes in the air?"

Agnes MacGowan shook her head and laughed. And added that in the great era of tranquillity opening before them all each could devote himself to appropriate constructive work in binding up the nation's wounds. Terence O'Donovan, nearby, stirred from his reverie and saluted them with a vivacity in his generally reserved manner.

One could note an iron will in the deep and smouldering eyes, a force in the straight, pugnacious nose. There was a fundamental sincerity about the man, and when his eyes left at rare moments some distant horizon, they seemed to pierce all the disguises of the human soul. He chatted till Macken came up to take his leave.

"Damn O'Donovan!" said Macken with a sudden fury in the

street. "He's neither British nor Irish, Free State nor Republican, male nor female, but the Idea in Itself."

"True," said Harding. "Yet there is a touch of greatness about him and Considine and half a dozen others. Only half a dozen others, mind, no more. Quite capable of wrecking Ireland for a word, but for Ireland's sake, if they did not exist, we should have to invent them!"

"I would rather have Michael Collins's little finger!" snapped Macken, relapsing into a gloomy silence. But in Harding's mind the scales of the argument quivered still. The Irish people and their right to life, liberty and the pursuit of happiness? Or the dream Republic drilled and talked into them for five years?

At his desk one night the telephone bell rang; and the whisper of Death sounded in his ears, for even in times of war and revolution there are natural deaths. Stranger than the Death unveiled but once on long lists on the *Emancipator's* desks with Winifred Considine's name. Death changed from standing type to fading flesh and blood. Would David Harding come over to Thomas O'Dea? Sudden stroke. Little hope.

Thomas O'Dea lay dying in his great wooden bed in the little room above the bar where the best part of his life had been spent. His face was ashen, and he was semi-conscious. His hands gripped the rosary beads with which he had prayed for his relatives, his country and his trade for forty years. In the night the watchers heard him whisper: "A little longer, Lord, a little longer." But towards morning he sat upright, stretched out his hands and passed with a cry.

Michael Collins sent a wreath, and found time to attend the funeral, shaking his head in sadness over the unfilled grave. And as the long line of carriages rolled back from Glasnevin, David Harding felt that almost the last link with the Ireland he knew was broken. The scales of the balance ceased to quiver in his mind. He no longer listened to Republican or Free Stater or the puzzled Dubliners in vexed debate. A haunting incapacity for feeling grew into a numbing paralysis of thought. He looked at the great ships sailing out from the Bay, and wondered what he would find in the worlds beyond. All the enthusiasms of his youth were dead. So a-wandering again. Somewhere on the seas and five continents to brush the cobwebs from his brain. Ireland could do without him. Beneath the greyness of his mind and the sickness of his will only one spark of the old fires flickered. "Good-bye! Good-bye!" the presses sang to him as he listened to their farewell humming. "Good-bye, but the song is not finished yet. Stay awhile, see it out, hear it out, stick it out, good-bye, good-bye, good-bye!"

. . . . . .

A week later, Agnes MacGowan changed her mind. Arthur Macken, on a visit, laughed sagely when she declared: "A woman who cannot change her mind has no mind to change. I was mistaken about that rotten Treaty. Up the Republic!" Patrick Edward MacGowan, happiest of mortals, went on smoking his pipe.

"Kiss me, dear," said Agnes. "I must go round this evening and help to make Michael Collins's meeting in College Green lively. By the way things are going we shall probably spend next year in jail, and the rest of our lives there into the bargain." She showed the company a whistle and a clasp knife of formidable dimensions. "The first," she explained with enthusiasm, "is for Mick's specious arguments. The second is to remove any tricolours he attempts to display."

As Macken took his leave a sharp doubt came into his mind. A thousand exploits and devotions of these women danced in his thoughts. Agnes rising in the small hours to admit a hunted man . . . guns behind her walls . . . Easter fires . . . vanity or true instinct? Venom for midnight raiders. . . . Justice unknown to women. . . . Their turn now. . . . Tigers again . . . claws out.

"Too constant ever!" said Macken aloud, smiling. He strode back to his barracks, his hand gripping firmly an automatic revolver in his right-hand pocket.

CHAPTER XVII

SIX months later, David Harding tramped, tramped, tramped through a wild lonely mountainous district in the South, wondering at his green uniform, at Macken marching in front of the long column of Free State troops, and whether Considine, Terence O'Donovan and the Tiger Doyle, hidden somewhere in the shadows above, would catch him and his comrades in a trap. Everywhere Michael Collins was sweeping to victory and the new Invisible Army falling back before his impetuous rush onwards and sledge-hammer strokes. Here the Republicans were making their most serious stand. Driven from the capital and the larger towns, the Irregular forces now used against

Michael Collins the tactics and methods he had employed in the Little War.

On the eve of the day when Dublin had awakened to the roar of guns bombarding the Four Courts, Harding had passed through further physical and mental adventures. His bag had been packed in his little Drumcondra room and he had prepared to start his wanderings again. He had said farewell to Michael Kerrigan, received a pipe from Papa Shanahan and given a last look at the *Emancipator*. He said farewell to Macken, too, beneath his tricolour flapping proudly over the Dublin barracks and busy taking over amid the clang of telephone bells and the rumble of departing lorries and tenders packed with smiling Tommies and sullen Black and Tans.

Then on Dublin fell the furies of Civil War, not unannounced. One night, Dick Blake had told him: "We are split above in the mill like in the old days. A third gone home, a third with the Staters in brand-new uniforms, and the rest with Condron and Considine wanting the Republic and nothing less. Peace? We'll never have peace. The lads are holding on to their guns. The young ones are out posting up bills on the walls and trampoles."

Michael Kerrigan shook his head in the *Emancipator* office and pronounced: "They all hate us, though God knows without us the world would never have heard half of the agony of this country. Don't I know these blasted politicians? They think newspapers exist to publish their portraits and speeches, and when they are making the welkin ring with denunciation of us, you'll meet them on the backstairs of your own newspaper trying to wangle in a nice little par., and they think the poor reporter is responsible for everything in his own bloody paper, from misprints to leading articles. We'll be blown up by the wild fellows, and what's left over the British will finish off when they come back, and they'll be right, for we were the worst brake on their activities. Same old story. Ship at the harbour's mouth wrecked by faction. The old Party lasted thirty years, these fellows four, and now they're eating each other. I'd hang them all up on trees, so I would."

But Thomas P. Bolger stood on the rock of the Republic: "Michael, you are wrong. I say: 'Up the Irregs.!' And why? Well, their arguments are damned bad, and I wouldn't sleep with any of their female camp followers for all the wealth of India. Pro-Treaty husbands is what those lassies want! But when both the *Liberator* and the *Emancipator* are united against them, ten to one there's something to be said for the fellows."

"Aye, Thomas!" chuckled Michael. "We always back the wrong horse, but the *Liberator* always knows the way the wind is going to blow the day after tomorrow, and I do notice it has a leg dangling down the gunman's side of the fence."

The two became serious when Bolger said: "Civil War before summer! Only a miracle can avert it. Too well we know the signs of trouble. First a whisper and then the storm. How can the armed anti-Treaty crowd climb down after the speeches they've made? And the bitterness in the city this minute. And the bloody women setting the menfolk by the ears!"

Two nights later Harding was strolling down the quays towards Phoenix Park when he noticed a tricolour over the Four Courts, and groups of men erecting barbed-wire entanglements. Here and there, armed guards watched while tenders and motors hummed along the quays. The Irregulars were seizing positions throughout the city.

"Halt!" A revolver was levelled at his head, and a small group surrounded him. The Tiger Doyle and Dick Blake were among them. Half an hour's fierce argument followed.

"Join us, man!" urged the Tiger, waving his revolver, his eyes ablaze. "We're in the soup. Our only hope is to seize power and carry on the existing Republic before we're repudiated at a panic election. The politicians have betrayed us. . . . Oh, well, if you want to be a bloody coward, go home." And sent Harding back to Drumcondra guarded by Dick Blake. But not before Harding had snapped at him:

"Mick Collins will flatten your little crowd quicker than he flattened the Black and Tans. He has Ireland behind him, and you know it, because you are afraid to trust the electors. Once you agreed to a Truce and once the Treaty was signed, the Republic was very sick and died soon after. The man in the street prefers a live Free State to a dead Republic."

"The Republic is dead when I am dead. We took an oath to that effect. Let England remove her threat of war. Then we'll talk!"

"Did you ever swear to an alibi?"

"I would swear to anything in a foreign court on the wrong Bible," parried the Tiger, his eyes twinkling. "But an oath taken of your own free will is a sacred engagement. Still, I am not worrying about oaths and all that junk. I leave that to the cods and spouters in the Dail. I know that threequarters of our supporters are trash, as much trash as the majority behind your precious Free State. I am going to ram the Republic down their throats as it was rammed down mine in spite of all the trimmers and old women and job hunters in Ireland. Ten years of the Free State and we'll be a British province."

"Then the Irish people are not worth bothering about," answered Harding. "And they'll be less worth bothering about if a handful of gunmen can terrorise them. What about the sufferings of the people? Why don't you leave it to the will of the people?"

"Will of your grandmother!" roared the Tiger. "Don't you try to put that rubbish across me. The fear of the people you mean. Fear of the return of the Black and Tans, fear of loss of jobs, fear of wounds and death, fear of the British! Will of the tree-tops that bend to the strongest breeze! Was Nineteen Sixteen the will of the people? Haven't they chopped and changed ever since you can remember them? The Republic is worth everything—suffering, terror, war, defeat. And we'll beat your damned Free State by destruction! Clear off, you ——"

And the Tiger's words set Harding alight. An hour before his mind had been cynical and detached. A tenderness for the Republic still lingered deep down inside him. A spark beneath the ashes broke into flame. He snarled:

"I bet you five pounds to a farthing that Mick Collins wipes the floor with you inside a month, that the people round on you like they rounded on the Black and Tans, and that I join the Free State in the morning!"

"Done!" said the Tiger. "Ten pounds to five I give. Now go to Hell. But if I thought that you were going to join the enemy forces, I'd lock you up here, so I would."

As they walked to Drumcondra, past the different positions the Irregulars had seized and the turmoil in the streets and the excited crowds outside many buildings with tricolours floating and young men striding up and down brandishing revolvers, Dick Blake confessed his innermost thoughts:

"Do you know why I am where I am? Looking for what the rest of Ireland wants and can't have: peace and a quiet time! The young one at home has me daft, and Agnes MacGowan and the rest of them Cumann na mBan wagging their tongues, night, noon and morning! Begod, I'd rather be with the Tiger waiting for Mick Collins to swoop on us or back in Frongoch itself."

"Leaves in the wind!" thought Harding. "No free will in times like these. This movement has to run its course. Revolutions are like that. Which of us is right? Does it matter?"

Next morning, to Macken's surprise, Harding walked in and

told him he had joined the new army. Macken listened to his story and smiled.

"The Tiger knows how to fight, but he's beaten before he's fired a shot. But one thing he does not know: human nature, and especially Irish human nature. He thinks he can terrorise and rush it. But there's a limit to taunts, and it's second nature to us to resist."

Then Macken looked away and, pointing in the Four Courts direction, continued: "Civil War! What happened between the Tiger and you is happening now in every county in Ireland. What do they mean? There are negotiations going on this minute, and they have agreed to surrender all their positions except what you see beneath that dome under the tricolour yonder. And we are playing a game of chess with each other. But nothing will come of it. It will all run its course now. Force to force. . . . We should have attacked long ago. Shootings on both sides already. Then reprisals and ambushes and executions and disillusion. . . . And the British won't be patient for ever. . . . Don't forget that."

The storm broke. All too rapidly Harding watched the hissing, lurid, hateful reels of tragedy flashed on the national screen.

First he saw the *Emancipator* a mass of leaping amber flames, as in Nineteen Sixteen he had seen the General Post Office. The *Emancipator*, with its machines sledge-hammered and its familiar rooms petrol-soaked, and its staff chased into the streets at the revolver's point, as he had seen the Black and Tans chase sub-editors, reporters and printers. With the Free State troops who were rushed to the building next morning he examined the wreckage. His eye caught a charred Irregular manifesto among the blackened wood and twisted printing presses.

"Whereas," the document ran, "by virtue of the powers conferred on me, Commandant . . . commanding . . . hereby give notice to all whom it may concern. . . ." He nodded to Michael Kerrigan, who haunted the ruins with an empty despair in his eyes, and looked away to the mourning group of printers and others standing as witnesses to the ruin of a world. So this was the final note of the machines. Ah! Had he known! "Whereas." The word infuriated him. So they copied the jargon as well as the methods of their enemies!

Their enemies. . . . Another hideous reel flashed on the screen. Michael Collins, in a side-street near the Four Courts, watching pallid, firm-lipped and with a sad distant look in his eyes, the guns which roared and thundered at the Irregular strongholds across the river. . . . Force to force. . . . Blow

142

for blow. . . . A watching Dublin crowd at the bridges below regulated by burly policemen and applauding impartially the roaring guns and angry volleys which replied, and tap-tap-tap and Boom, Boom, Boom, just as in Nineteen Sixteen.

Just as in Nineteen Sixteen. Again barricaded windows, volleys, cannonade, cordons closing in and men caught in a trap, tunnelling desperately through the walls while the smoke and flames leaped skywards from the heart of Dublin and with a sullen roar of bursting land mines the Irregulars surrendered and were marched to the prisons that Michael Collins now ruled.

Through Ireland swept the flame of Civil War. As Harding dashed through the streets in a lorry, he recalled the street ambushes which had set his heart and nerves a-jump. From the roofs the Irregular snipers were active. Twice he saw men sink to death with a moan beside him, and twice bombs crashed behind his lorry with the sharp accompaniment of rattling revolvers. . . . Men lying dead on the cobble-stones like Bernard Milroy, oh, so long ago. . . .

And this war was fought fiercely without pride or courtesy or glimpses of grandeur which lights war betimes. And already a dark chronicle of murder was whispered abroad. Whispers yet which may not grow, for the Irregular resistance weakened and the end of war was in sight as Michael Collins struck, and negotiated and struck again. Victoriously through the South he marched at the head of his army, and the flame of Civil War burned lower. And David Harding was wondering as he marched and tramped under the shadows of the lonely hills in the South where it was all going to end.

A motor-cycle swept round the bend of the road, and close behind came a large car, a tender of Free State troops and an armoured car. The column cheered. Michael Collins shouted a greeting from the large car as he and his escort dashed past. "Always carried his life in his hand," thought Harding. "Wiser if he remained in Dublin, with the Tiger crouching among those hills."

But that night the Tiger purred. The column had halted at a small village in the early evening. Sentries had been posted, and the sun was falling over the glorious silver river, restful green woods and purple hills. Macken sent a messenger to Harding. Macken was smiling. He handed Harding a note. It was in the Tiger's scrawling hand and also counter-signed with Considine's bold signature, proposing a truce and inviting Macken to a parley among the hills.

"We can trust Considine's word," said Macken. "I have made all arrangements."

They passed the sentries and went up winding paths deeper and deeper into the sombre hills. Macken whispered as he observed Harding's questioning look:

"This truce talk is all poppy-cock. Considine and the Tiger are lonely. We are only going to talk about old times, but there will be no fighting until our return. I wish Mick were here. He might talk them over in this mood. Things have gone well with us lately, and unless ——"

A low whistle sounded above. The party halted, and the Tiger ran down to shake hands with Macken. He led them into a deep cave in which a large fire was blazing. At a small table laid for supper Considine was seated in a weather-worn uniform. He was reading, and smiled gravely. Terence O'Donovan stepped from the back of the cave and saluted Macken with a mock formality.

"You ought to have a star after your name, Terry!" said Macken. "As you told me and Harding on a famous occasion." And for two hours these men forgot the Civil War or that they might fall by each other's hands on the morrow. The Tiger Doyle sang gaily, and his audience shook the hills with the ringing chorus of his favourite song:

> Hey-ho, the rattling bog,
> The bog down in the valley O!

To tales of the days before the Civil War then, and the Tiger asked courteously for Michael Collins, and added:

"War is war. But let's hope that none of us meet during this little scrap and that nothing happens to Mick, although he will make himself a walking target, trusting to the Devil's luck. But he wouldn't be the man he is if he didn't carry on the like of that. Do you remember, Arthur, the day I was lying in the hospital in Dublin with three bullets in me? And the hunchbacked spy the lads had winged in the next bed to me, still up to his dirty tricks in spite of his wounds! He sent word to the Tans about myself, the last word he ever sent, by the way, for the lads called in to see him soon after and shot him like a dog in the yard. But I got wind, too, of his low tricks, and passed through the door just two minutes before the Tan tenders rolled up to the hospital. Outside was Mick waiting. He had seen those devils enter the street as he was passing, and organised a rescue on the spur of the moment—him the most-wanted man in Dublin! And he drove the jaunting car he commandeered past them with a flick of his whip and the hat the jarvey lent him on the back of his head, staring at them like a brainless old cow. He saved my life that day. They'd have had me otherwise."

"Mick has too much heart," broke in Terence O'Donovan. "He used to weep, as near to weeping as a man can get, anyway, when he heard of the children born mad in the Terror. Do you remember, Harding, the tale you told of the time he watched outside Mountjoy Jail, when the three lads were hanged within. Well, do you know he was to lead the rescue the day before, only someone blundered?"

"Yes," said Harding. "There he stood among the praying crowds with candles in their hands, and the armoured cars patrolling and the Tommies on guard."

"And then he came back," said Considine. "And the tears rolling down his cheeks, and not a word out of him but: 'Perhaps it was better for them,' and he made Dublin quake that night. He was in that mood, too, when his mother's house in these parts was burned, and his young brothers and sisters had to wander over the hills in the darkness. But there were more than tears in his eyes that night!"

"Mick has a heart all right," said the Tiger. "Remember, Harding, the night we went racing South to save Mrs. Lavelle? And if I was late that night, he saved many others time and again—including the big Black and Tan from myself. Oh, that was touch and go!"

"A great fighter and organiser," reflected Considine aloud. "Do you remember him at Havensfield? Filling up those canisters and screwing down those rude bombs? It never satisfied him any more than the volumes of poetry I was so foolish as to press on him! When he came out after the Rising, he laughed at the old haunts, and never rested until he had brighter and better bomb factories all over the city. He was critical of and outgrew his earlier handiwork!"

"Yes," agreed Terence O'Donovan. "But the greatest thing he ever did was to get his eyes and ears inside the Castle, and into every barracks in Ireland. And the money he raised. No one man could have done one of those things better than he did, but he did them all."

"If we only had had time to think," murmured Considine. "This tragedy might have been averted . . . time to allow for each other's opinions . . . but, no, each in his little corner. . . . No, still those were the times. And nothing will be as black as we fear. . . . And the Republic will be worth it all."

Song and talk again until the darkness deepened.

"We'll call the bet off, Harding," said the Tiger amicably. "Your month's time limit is up, but you fellows have given us a run for our money. I'm game to fight till I drop, unlike those fellows who surrendered in the West last week, a hundred of them, rifles and machine-guns, and the Devil knows what else, and not a scratch or a black eye among them. That's what I meant when I mentioned trash, Harding. Wish I'd been there!"

"You are not much use for anything but fighting, Tiger Doyle!" said Macken. And they parted, leaving Terence O'Donovan with a gonfalon in his eyes, Considine with his dream and the Tiger Doyle ready to fight till he dropped. Then on the national screen—for to Harding this time had all the unreality of some clicking and hideous film play—flashed a scene, forerunner of scenes grimmer and more terrible yet.

The Civil War slackened, starred by the ambushes which flickered and gleamed in the wake of Michael Collins and his forward rush. Deeper and more surely into the hills his forces pressed, while every day that passed, his Irregular opponents drifted homewards, dumping their well-oiled rifles.

Macken chatted to Harding a week after their strange meeting with Considine and the Tiger Doyle.

"Near the end, thank Heaven!" he was saying. "If we could only catch or persuade the Tiger, we could end the war. They can't win now. The country has kicked. They have made their stand, and if they continue they will raise a savage feeling against them. Why, even in Dublin now, there are staid citizens, howling at the army to take no more prisoners. Considine and O'Donovan know when they are beaten. The Tiger never does."

"I doubt that," said Harding. "Terence's visions are more bloody than the Tiger's guns——"

The column was resting and the sun was sinking over the sombre hills above. A motor-cycle swept round the bend of the road, and Michael Collins's car and escort drew up beside the column.

Mick jumped down and hastened towards Macken. His eyes were keen and thoughtful. He was smiling, but an abstracted look passed over his face. He nodded to the troops, shouting: "How goes it, boys?" Reports were handed to him. He read them quickly and asked for news of Irregular forces in the neighbourhood.

"We have news of large bodies observed some miles ahead," said Macken. "O'Donovan is supposed to have fallen back and reformed his column. But in this quarter things are quiet."

"Good," said Mick. "It's all over but the shouting. And

146

some very bloodthirsty shouting there is in Dublin these times. No bloody use to the country. Well, good-bye! I'll move on towards Cork. I am going back to Dublin tomorrow. My work is done."

"Don't be so reckless!" protested Macken. "If you must go I will have to increase your escort. Wait here till morning, at any rate. The last reports made me uneasy. I can't answer for your safety two miles farther on."

"Stow it, you windy bastard!" cried Mick in high good humour. "As if anyone asked you to answer for anything, you gouger! Did I have an escort when I was the most-hunted man in Ireland, with ten thousand pounds on my head? Cut out all that bloody talk! If I am to be shot, I am to be shot!"

He looked away into the darkening countryside, his grey-blue eyes alight with a fun in curious contrast to the violence of his tone. His eyes mirrored changing moods. The vivid smile faded and a grave, weary, defiant and sorrowful expression settled on his face. Grey-blue burned to a sombre amber. He spoke quietly and almost deferentially to Macken:

"Sorry, Arthur. Don't worry yourself. Queer things happen in life. But I shall hardly be shot down here in my own county. That would be too much. Good-bye. See you in Dublin."

Macken watched him uneasily as he strode to his car. Why would Mick be so obstinate and fatalistic when all hopes of victory hung on his life? He should have remained in Dublin. Nice Commander-in-Chief, careering round the hills for the enemy to take pot-shots at him.

The motor-cycle disappeared in the darkness, followed by Mick's car, the tender of troops and armoured car. Down the road Macken heard Mick shouting cheerfully to the column as he passed.

Macken knitted his brow. A motor-cycle hummed in the distance, and one of his scouts saluted. He breathed again and reproached himself for his fears: no movements of Irregulars reported. Mick had the best of the time with that obstinate refusal to remember personal danger. And yet? Another half-hour. . . . A motor-cycle roared in the distance, and one felt the infection of fear in the strident and furious howling of the engine. A pale-faced soldier dashed towards Macken, eyes burning with excitement, his face streaked with dust and blood. Into the silence of the camp a terror came. And faintly in the distance volleys sounded, and the splutter of machine-gun fire. Silence and the faint rifle echoes once more.

As the lorries tore along the road to the rescue, winding and

147

speeding in the darkness, Harding felt a foreboding which deepened to certainty. He had not much time for reflection, for fire was opened on all sides, and the leading lorry was held up by felled trees blocking the main road. Machine-guns and searchlights whipped and stabbed the darkness. Half an hour of furious effort and the lorries rolled on to the heavy volleying below. Explosions shook the air, and the volleys wakened the hillsides. As the lorries approached, the firing slackened and died. Again obstructions on the road and rifles spitting and flashing in the darkness.

The attackers faded away. A solitary shot echoed down the slopes, where Michael Collins was fighting for his life—two miles from his mother's blackened ruin of a house.

Macken hastened forward. He found an armoured car with jammed guns, a battered tender and nearby Michael Collins's great car, speckled with bullet marks. Some yards to the left, Michael Collins lay dead, a rifle in his hands, a bullet through his brain. He had died, a melancholy group of officers told Macken, firing to the last, while bombs and bullets hurtled round him. As the attack slackened, and the attackers fled to the hills, a stray bullet caught him, and with a sigh he sank to the ground—and never spoke again.

Often had Macken seen him sleeping thus, a vigour in his quiescent features. Again in Macken's ears stray bullets sounded: Moore Street, Nineteen Sixteen and the doomed Volunteers waiting the word to break themselves against Maxwell's cordons, against that barricade with its khaki watchers, outside machine-guns and thousands ready around and in the rear. In a corner, Michael Collins brooding, as broken as the Tiger Doyle looking down on his dead brother earlier in the week, Michael Collins with that deepening look of horror as the riddled, spinning, inert corpses of those civilians dead an hour ago at the foot of the impregnable barricade are pierced, stagger and stiffen again and again in the brain of Michael Collins. His face growing paler, paler, paler—paler than it lies in repose even now. Horror deepening to horror in his eyes. Muttering to himself and huddling to himself at every distant shot. . . . A moan of defeat from his lips. . . . Macken speaking and Mick's face clearing as he sits up again with leaden impassive features to wait for the end. . . . Not the end. An oak henceforward when the strongest are levelled by howling hurricanes. . . . In that hour fear had died in the soul of Michael Collins. . . . Frongoch and Mick speaking: "Rule Ireland or we will die." Pictures, gay, grim and casual until the end. Michael Collins dead in the heart of his native hills, the lights of his great car burning, a broken and silent group gazing down on the dead Dictator . . . who had held and ruled Ireland, and died. "Queer things happen in life."

Victory lay there. A sigh rose from the group and went round Ireland. Seven days later, three hundred thousand mourners wept as Michael Collins's coffin was borne with military pomp through the Dublin streets. . . . And Macken and Harding, as they tramped behind, had brains of lead and eyes of glass.

Brains of lead and eyes of glass as the cortege, three miles long, moved swiftly with its army of wreath-laden, crepe-draped lorries, its seventeen bands moaning Handel's Funeral March, its Archbishops and Bishops in solemn canonical robes, its advance guard of cavalry, its Generals, Captains and grey-green firing party, fifty strong, with rifles reversed, and buglers in the rear, its mourners afoot and in coaches, file after file of working men, clerks, students, clergymen, women, officials, all passing swiftly in the wake of the coffin on an eighteen-pounder gun-carriage drawn by six sable horses. The sun pouring down on six miles of spectators as the procession flashed by with mournful pride to Glasnevin, where O'Connell's lime-white Round Tower soared sentinel to the newest comer and comrade in the Irish Pantheon.

Mourners afoot, mourners lining the streets, mourners on the roofs, with the sun pouring down and the silence of doom over all as the Funeral March stops and Dublin follows, looks on in wondering heartache and stupefied anger, sobs quietly and pays a last homage to Michael Collins in his coffin drawn by six sable horses to an eternal sleep in the heart of his nation, dark hair quiescent now, vibrating accent stilled and determined jaw set for ever.

. . . .

Grimmer and darker pictures flashed on the screen. Macken, back in the South, swept through the hills, avoiding all the Tiger's traps. Once Harding remembered marching for hours. Body for body of Free State troops joined the column: men in uniform, men half in uniform, men who had fought the Black and Tans, men who had fought at the Dardanelles and in Flanders, men who had known all the wars at home and abroad, a marching, singing, shouting section of the fifty thousand troops now hounding the Republicans to defeat while the new rulers in Dublin planned and hoped in their barbed-wired and stoutly fortified offices—fifty thousand troops sweeping into the towns and villages and swooping in in ships on the coast towns and driving the Irregulars before them.

The Irregular flight into the hills grew, except in Dublin, where sullen land mines howled outside Government offices, and snipers fired across the roofs at their grey-green targets moving in the streets below, and if civilians got in the way, so much the worse for civilians. Bombs crashed behind lorries. But the Governmental grip tightened. Raids in the big towns and the Free State Army sweeping their enemies before them. Day by day the Irregulars sped from the villages into the remoter hills, or returned furtively to their homes, dumping, dumping, dumping their arsenals in bogs, in the walls of farmhouses, or in rough dug-outs, muttering: "Worse than the Terror. Worse than the Black and Tan times. Everyone is against us. Whom can we trust?" Small parties of the retreating Republicans mined the roads or sniped the growing Free State forces in sporadic ambushes.

And on this autumn evening, as Harding tramped ahead, he was thinking of the scene when he had gone on a peace parley to Considine and Terence O'Donovan only two nights ago. Words and words and words had passed in the small cottage where they had met, and Macken had shrugged his shoulders on his return.

The Tiger Doyle had been dark and silent. Considine had spoken but little. Terence O'Donovan had done all the talking, as haunted now by his dream Republic as he had been haunted by Michael Collins when Harding had met him in Galway on leave from the wars. And his eyes still seemed to search the horizon for something he would never find, as tragic and as granite as ever. And brushing aside Macken's offer to let him and his comrades go free if they laid down their arms and went home, Terence O'Donovan said that the Republic still lived and would be maintained so long as life remained in their veins. . . . So back to war and this tramping column.

Body after body of Free State troops swelled the ranks. A land mine exploded beneath the lorry in front of Harding. Angry Free State soldiers pursued the attackers, swearing savagely and waking the dying echoes with wilder and wilder volleys. Beside the gaping hole in the road lay the wrecked lorry and a mass of groaning and dying men. A man at Harding's side sank with a sigh, a jagged red star in his forehead. A rattle of revolver fire, the reports of rifles, and the murderous bursting of bombs and the answering fire into the roadsides which

150

sheltered the ambushers. Grey-green forms staggering to a bloody stillness and a glimpse of the flying Irregulars. . . .

The troops returned with four prisoners who shouted despairingly and defiantly: "Yes, we are Republicans. But we took no part in the ambush." They had been captured in a cottage, unarmed, a mile away. The attackers had fled long before and the four prisoners belonged to the growing number from the Irregular forces now drifting homewards. The march was resumed. All at once shots were heard from the rear. Rushing back, Harding saw the four prisoners lying dead on the roadside. "Shot while trying to escape." Ancient and familiar excuse. . . . Grimmer and darker and even more sordid.

A lonely farmhouse and a double ring of grey-green uniforms and flashes from the windows and red flames roaring. Five men surrendering while a defiant face with hard dark eyes gleaming scowls through the flames and a revolver spits and cracks and finds its billets. The roof crashes and the grey-green rings of men fall back and suspend their fire. The Tiger Doyle dashing towards them, firing as he runs. . . . He falls fighting and riddled with bullets, albeit cheated of death. . . . One sombre ray of the spirit in that Civil War which again, as on the eve of Michael Collins's passing, sinks lower and lower. . . . Terence O'Donovan surprised and made prisoner in his sleep as he lies in a hiding-place after his column has broken up and gone home. . . . And the blood howl rises in Dublin as the beaten Irregulars break and run. . . . Considine captured next and then court martialled and charged with possession of arms. . . .

Grimmer and darker and ever more sordid as the passions of the Civil War reveal themselves in dead men behind ditches and the midnight raids of the Irregulars to send houses blazing to the heavens and bridges crashing in reprisal for the unofficial executions which dot ditches with dead men or the wild savagery which binds captured Irregulars to land mines and blows them to atoms. . . .

In one blinding and lurid flash Harding saw the end of the picture commenced for him when the Irish Volunteers marched to their drill hall on the quays and into insurrection. . . . And he saw it, too, in the very Dublin barracks where he had told Macken of his answer to the Tiger's challenge.

As the dawn stole through the windows of the room where Arthur Macken and David Harding had kept an all-night vigil, a clock away in the great city sounded. Sounds of morning approaching could be heard in the distance—a circle of crowing cocks, faint peaceful murmurs lapsing to a deadly stillness. Harding could hear his heart-beats keeping time to the racing tick, tick, tick of his watch. Macken's face was pale and tense, his eyes blood-shot; a mournful smile stole across his firm lips but through his eyes a procession of horrors passed: a journey through an Inferno of Memories, memories crowding fast, six months of Hell since Dublin had awakened to the roar of the guns bombarding the Four Courts, and Civil War had swept through Ireland like a flame. Flashes of grandeur and nobility had lighted a sordid struggle, past comradeship peered out of even the mouth of Hell.

Hell, yes, Hell. Here in this barracks he had passed in only eight months before, with the tricolour floating over it, and the British Commandant taking a stiff and courteous farewell of his old stronghold, meticulous and self-possessed amid rumours, tension and alarms. Black and Tans had driven past him as he entered the gates. Green-uniformed Irish soldiers were moving through the squares and rooms amidst the chaos of arrival and the clang of telephone bells. . . .

A fresh-faced young man in green, very fresh-faced, smiling, eager, lounged against a wall, wonder in face and bearing. The young man smiled at him, interrupting his reverie with: "It's great!" Charming illusion of youth! "It's great!" repeated the young man, pointing after the Black and Tan lorries lumbering through the gates. "Those fellows looked at us with Hell in their eyes!" But let them look today, back to his reverie of youth then, gazing at the flapping tricolour. . . . A June vision flashed into Macken's whirling brain. The same youthful dreamer regulating a crowd in a Dublin street. Shots and a man retreating with Hell in his eyes. The youthful dreamer weltering in a pool of blood on the pavement. Panic and curses and shrieks. Hell in eyes you did not expect, young dreamer! Hell on the walls, too. Huge flaring legends of rage and hate in blaring white paint. Huge white letters which howled with demon voices:

SHOVE UP IN YOUR GRAVE, MICHAEL COLLINS, AND MAKE ROOM FOR THE REST OF THE TRAITORS.

Suspicion and apathy brooding over the people. The bottom blown clean out of the beliefs of thousands. Rogues, looters, wasters and hysterical women wrapping petty crimes and private griefs in the tricolour, too soon dyed red in the blood of the brothers of yesterday.

Away in the South, only a week ago, grim orders from Dublin had sent Terence O'Donovan to join Michael Collins. Falling at an execution post at the hands of his own countrymen. Terence O'Donovan shaking hands with the firing party, smiling courteously. . . . He had fallen with his eyes on his distant horizon, saying he died for Truth and Ireland and all such have no need of prayer. . . .

The morning light grew brighter. Macken did not move. A sound of rifles clanking on bare ground, the dull rattle of spades, voices. . . . Half an hour more. . . . Harding pondered, too, smoking innumerable cigarettes.

And Harding, in particular, the laughing confident face of Michael Collins rose to haunt. Like a mocking refrain through his thoughts went the words of the old heroic tale:

"An awesome Spectre, forbidding in looks, a Fearsome One, like a ferocious Devil-Giant, Fionn saw, and he going through the gloomy and tangled wood. . . . A Drab Coat was wrapped about him with mud-beplastered skirts, his tremendous brogues thundering like mighty waves every pace he strode. . . . But when the Churl of the Drab Coat came from the ship to the place where Fionn and his warriors stood, lo! the wind and the sun flamed before and behind, and they saw then 'twas MANANNAN MAC LIR, Fairy Phantom of Rathcroghan, who had come to save them in the dire strait in which they were."

Wind and sun . . . dire strait.

Incongruous and irrelevant details simmered and subsided in Macken's brain, too. Condron joking in the mill. Poor old mill. It was a hopeless ruin now since Dick Blake and a few others had blown it sky high to prevent it being occupied by Free State forces. . . . Books, thrills, shootings, dances, and a dream-like phantasmagoria of trees, flowers, scenes of his childhood, the night he had lain wounded in the Dublin home, the Tiger swearing as he raided the railway carriage, a description by a countryman in Frongoch of the Rising in County Galway and their Captain, Sean Condron's brother, sitting under the trees like in the pictures, begod, and fellows galloping up on horses and saluting and a cruiser shelling the woods from the Bay, escape to America. Great man. . . . Sean a great man, too. Ran in the family like a wooden leg. What had someone said in the Dail debate on the Treaty, close to his ear in that damned tiresome debate? Condron rising, eloquent amidst an attentive hush. A trifle arrogant, lean figure alert and taut and great grey eyes alive under his bushy brow. Glaring at Mick.

"Yes," the voice at Macken's ear had said, "if that man took me out to shoot me in the morning, I should still respect him as sincere." Drill mad. Knew every part of a gun. Wounded

Nineteen Sixteen and going strong since. Guiding the city ambushes. Grimmer than Considine. No. Yes. Easter spectre goading him on, and yet not his fault when the arms landing failed. Motives of men. Others see them, not themselves. The Tiger, too. One minute in the thick of the Rising and he might have been the Lamb Doyle for duration. Fine pub the Lamb Doyle's. No, Dick Blake drank pints there on Sundays, and Dick was no lamb. Dick had escaped so far. Old dog for the hard road and the pup for the path. Go away to America and forget it all. Voted for Murder Bill. Yes, they called it that. Shock Ireland, he had said. Save Ireland. Hadn't they issued amnesties till the printers were tired? Lay down your arms. Go home. Nothing easier. Irregulars had killed the Republic for fifty years. It did not matter. They were all going, Mick . . . Terence . . . all of them . . . and not by the hands they expected, but by their own. . . . Harding looking pale yonder. . . . Two files of men with rifles levelled. Doing their job. Shocking Ireland. Saving Ireland.

A clock struck outside. As the last strokes died away, a volley roared below the windows in the yard. A century passed, and Harding's face turned a ghastly pallor. Macken gazed in front of him. A second volley. Sean Condron and Dermot Considine lay dead in the yard.

An officer entered to confirm the news. "Vengeance they will call it," muttered Macken. "Vengeance? Shock Ireland. Save Ireland." He fell swooning to the floor.

The words of the old heroic tale droned in Harding's ears, and he thought: "What are words and tales in an hour like this?"

CHAPTER XVIII

SMALL bands of Irregulars still held out among the hills or lay hidden in the Dublin cellars or crept into sympathisers' at midnight for food and rest and clothing. But the Civil War was fading and the demobilisation of the warring forces had commenced. David Harding took off his green coat at length to go back to a world where faith, hope and charity were fast asleep. One thought beat through his brain: NOTHING ON EARTH WAS WORTH IT. In spite of victory, in spite of Michael Collins, in spite of the tricolour waving over three of Ireland's four green fields, in spite of the moist and mellow Dublin nights and days with their promise of eternal re-birth dimming with Nature's splendour all the transient rages and pranks of mankind.

He wanted one thing only: to forget. All feeling was numbed. The beliefs of a lifetime swayed and crashed and reeled to death. Friendship had gone as the volleys of firing parties crashed and spades clanked to open gaping graves. NOTHING ON EARTH WAS WORTH IT. The tricolour drooped mournfully over Dublin Castle, but Dublin's Fair City was no longer fair. The very children no longer sang, and suspicion and aching silence fell over the brooding crowds. In the days of Civil War the heart of Ireland had grown numb. As the toll of executions mounted, the people shrugged their shoulders and asked: "Oh, four more men shot? Another fellow dead in a ditch? Another house burned down? Children, too. Well, well." And many honest folk summed up their feelings thus: "You can trust no one! Indeed, you might well be suspicious of yourself."

It was the hour of reaction, of the place-hunter, the intriguer, the hopeless, the mediocre, the superstitious. Beneath the debris the spirit of the Irish Revolution was buried. Where was there light? Would Ireland be great again in their generation, or some new movement rise, revolutionary, religious, social or literary? And to David Harding and a hundred thousand others it seemed not. Never had the pride and self-respect of a nation been so deeply wounded.

Anything to forget. He wandered through the city, looking for a gleam of the old fairness and the old glamour, but the citizens were only happy when they prayed in the great noble churches or drugged themselves in the small ignoble pubs. One evening he went back to Thomas O'Dea's old Family Grocery, under new management, which still set the clocks by the comings and goings of the old stagers. He went out quickly, for the place was peopled with ghosts: Bernard Milroy, Terence O'Donovan, Thomas O'Dea and Michael Collins. He shut his eyes, and their faces rose in a hundred scenes.

He passed out into the labyrinth of streets which composed the darkest quarter of the underworld of Dublin, the cancer no revolutionary surgeon's knife had ever cut. Past the pitiful and bedraggled procession of the streets he strode, heavy in brain and foot, on and on. Blatant faces, strident voices, slouching and drunken mortals, darkened stairways, garbage heaps, oaths, blows, disease-laden and fetid winds, pubs with garish lights, everywhere poverty, everywhere a remittent and feverish squalor, everywhere women crouching, loitering and offering themselves for sale, disappearing down alley-ways or into houses with their prey. Sometimes a bloated and pox-fretten visage was thrust into his face, and an obscene invitation hurled to him with alcohol-laden breath and adenoidal whine: overhead the stars shone above this Inferno. Through his thoughts beat the unending refrain, goading him to madness and death: NOTHING ON EARTH WAS WORTH IT. . . . "Patroclus died that far passed thee. . . ." A scenario of horrors in his memory to that chorus of sodden and perambulating strumpets. . . . Ireland—empty word.

At a street corner, a young woman loitered, bedecked and hovering. She grabbed his arm with a weary and lecherous wail: "Good night, deary. Come along with me, love?" Lights blazed from the adjacent three-storey brothel. Glasses clinked and a voice howling a hilarious litany of blasphemy and filth. A man with bullet head and blood-shot eyes stood on guard at the door. In the darkness beyond, the heels of beshawled harpies prowling beat metallically on the pavements. Harding laughed, and at the madness in his eyes the young woman drew back and fled shrieking. . . . Escape. . . . Escape. . . . Escape from this maddening: NOTHING ON GOD'S EARTH WAS WORTH IT. Sin-eaten spectres wailed and vanished. Something wrong with his brain. The arguments went round and round. Tomorrow away over the Bay to cool his thoughts.

"Hello, David!" said a familiar voice, and the Tiger Doyle stepped from the darkness. His face was pale and pinched, and his eyes sunken and spiritless. His boots were broken and his clothes ragged. His head and hands were rudely bandaged. The Tiger spoke tersely:

"I escaped from the military hospital a week ago and fled here. I heard if I recovered it was all u.p. with me, so I took no chances. Escaped on my own. Couldn't get in touch with the lads. I have slept in archways and empty houses. Nowhere to hide."

The Tiger's plight brought Harding to his senses. "Pull yourself together," he said. "The war is wellnigh over, all but the shouting. Come home and I'll hide you all right."

Through back-lanes the Tiger limped with Harding to Drumcondra, and lay unconscious the whole day following. When he awoke that evening Harding had clothes and money ready for him, and the news in the evening papers of the "cease-fire" order issued by the Republican leaders. The Tiger sat in silence for a long time before he spoke:

"A good thing the Civil War has been called off. It would have drifted into a series of private vendettas and family feuds. So it is over and I am alive. I don't care what happens now.

Ever since my brother was killed I've looked for death, but somehow it's missed me. And I had meant to go down fighting. We made in this Civil War every mistake that men could make: fighting on our enemy's ground, in our enemy's time and with the people against us——"

"So Mick was right?" asked Harding. "You should have taken the Treaty?"

"No!" said the Tiger shortly. "We should not. We should never have allowed the Civil War to take place. We should have gone home and waited until the Irish have all the faults and all the virtues of the English. But why talk? Mick was nearly a great man, but he's dead now, and he was never great enough to face the British at the council table."

"Who was then?" asked Harding. "And tell me this. If you think the British fooled us, what guarantee have you if you had won the Civil War or if you win over the people to your side again, that you won't be fooled again, fooled for ever and ever?"

The Tiger's face twitched sharply.

"That is not a fair question," he said simply.

"Do you remember what O'Donovan said on the eve of his execution in his farewell letter: that the majority of us had lost ourselves in the routine of the struggle and lost sight of principles, of history's lessons, of an intellectual basis, of the real re-conquest of not only the liberties but the lands of Ireland? That was an echo of Considine. Why, then, did two such men ever go into a Civil War?"

"Birds of a feather!" laughed the Tiger. "You mean you are sorry we are not talking yet. Mick and I were worth the lot of you. Well, you can talk for the next ten years, and I hope you enjoy the company you will find yourself in."

"Thanks!" said Harding. "But I am going on my travels for the next ten years."

"Hope things are better by the time I see you again," said the Tiger.

They talked till midnight, arguing and evoking ghosts. Then the Tiger, a subdued gleam in his eye, shook hands with Harding and went into the darkness slowly.

. . . .

Over Dublin the shadows lifted as the Civil War became a memory. Howth stood out as starkly as ever in the dim and winding Bay. Sunlight bathed the great city whence to any watcher on the sky-crowned and blunt-topped hills or on the ships gliding inwards or outwards still came that low and almost inaudible hum, a promise of El Dorado. The children sang in the streets and played round the new buildings, leaping up from the debris and wreckage in the heart of Dublin. The ache in the hearts of the citizens had died, too, and in their thousands they thronged the footpaths to raise welkin-shaking cheers, whenever pageants passed gorgeous with uniforms and cars. And the Dubliners' old acid wit and enthusiasm flowed and splashed and gleamed again around the platforms of politicians returned with the normal to recite legends and litanies.

Dublin's moist and mellow nights and days grew vivid with the glittering speech of the citizens, their eloquent, jolly, critical, slipshod, cordial, vinegar-tongued selves again.

"Listen to that old fellow blathering over there!" roars an orator to the delighted crowds. He extends a menacing finger towards the opposition platform. "Listen to the undemobilised warrior facing the bullets that have stopped flying and bawling for the Republic he never as much as crossed the road to get! Who is he? Where was he in the troubled times?"

"In the feathers, under the bed, bejaney!" roars the enraptured crowd. Michael Kerrigan takes down every word to be printed off on the new machines inside the *Emancipator* office which has risen, Phoenix-like as ever, from the ashes, and upstairs Thomas O'Kane's pendulum eyes sway and tick, his arms whirl and tomorrow his seductive and enigmatical posters will sell thousands of copies of the paper. Papa Shanahan in a new suit and a volcano of a new pipe a-smoking faithfully records a very shattering litany of family history, statistics and personal prowess from the opposition platform, while the crowd eggs on both parties with tantalising asides:

"Now there'll be gas! That was a quare one!"

"Hit him, mister!"

"Answer the man! Never mind what he done. Were you under the bed or were you not?"

"Who robbed the old-age pensioners? Feathering your nests, the whole pack of yous!"

"Ah, come and have a pint. They'd give you a pain in your craw. Uncles, aunts, cousins and brothers-in-law washing their dirty linen in public."

"Jasus! You'd need an umbrella to listen in comfort to these lads, baptising the multitude with the sweat of their tongues!"

" 'Tis great gas, all the same, listening to them cutting the tripes out of each other!"

Thomas P. Bolger in the thick of it all has regained his cheerful foxy look, and will tell even more dazzling stories than before, when he rejoins Papa Shanahan later in the "Diamond Bar," though betimes he looks mournful, as if he is slightly bored at watching a play he has heard too often.

Then as the population pursues its way in crowded factories, shops, music-halls, churches, pawnshops and tenements more self-consciously and maliciously than elsewhere, Dick Blake strides citywards, hale and unchanged, and as humorous as ever, thinking of his little daughter's wedding a month ago, and of the wars and the long months he spent in an internment camp, and of the day when he too will sleep in Glasnevin and Dublin will go on just as before, and he won't be missed, and there'll be no blow-out for him the like of tomorrow's. . . .

. . . .

A day of pageantry had dawned for Dublin. And it was Harding's last day in Dublin, too. Tomorrow, the mailboat would bear him into the open sea, sadder than on that April evening when he and his comrades had sailed for a prison in the English Midlands, Dublin's domes, spires and lights dimming to the darkness of their hearts. In his reverie seethed the stabbing memories of the years. Civil War? One more milestone on the march of the Irish people back into lands and liberties. What of the blood and tears and wars? They had freed and exhausted Ireland: "Better the excess than the defect, better the more than the less."

In Grafton Street, Agnes MacGowan passed on the way to the *salon* she had revived since a weary-souled prison governor had bowed her out to freedom once more. Pensive, all life and colour, blue eyes agleam with mirth and vitality, she moved, thinking of that day's celebrations and of a last glimpse of Michael Collins, as he watched the great guns shelling the Irregular strongholds across the river; of Dermott Considine at her windows later, sharing with her the vigil Winifred had kept in Nineteen Sixteen. Patrick Edward MacGowan walked beside her, bulging portfolios under his arm. . . . Patrick Edward MacGowan, T.D., famous in the law courts for his defence of political prisoners, whose obituary Michael Kerrigan had already written for the *Emancipator's* "cemetery," whose portrait Thomas O'Kane often shoved into a relevant two columns after a breeze in the Dail or Law Courts.

From a side-street gleamed flamboyantly the posters of a Republican sheet. . . . Still at it! . . . In ten years cold-blooded historians, omniscient and very wise after the event, could make their audit. . . . "Other Romans would arise, heedless of a

159

soldier's name." . . . Sounds not arms, harmony, path to fame.
. . . Winifred's old joke . . . sounds not arms, arms not sounds. . . .

The fog in his brain lifted and the ache in his heart dulled,
for a new wind swept through the streets. He looked up. Long
gay lines of bunting spanned and crossed slumland and main
thoroughfare. Green, White and Orange fluttered in a universal
riotousness. Vaster and vaster flowed the human tide over the
Dublin streets. A forest of wreaths climbed with clinging and
multi-coloured kisses from the base of the monument unveiled
that day to Michael Collins to the proud and simple epitaph
on its granite centre. With the last phrases of the orator, the
tragedy and age-wise melancholy in the capital's stones awoke.
On guard nearby Arthur Macken stood, his face impassive.
Swords flashed to a fierce and quivering reverence, a volley
rolled, a bugle pealed a farewell—mournful, militant, trium-
phant. And over the long lines of men in grey-green uniforms
marching back to their barracks a silent tenseness fell.

Away in the vast human sea, David Harding saw for the last
time the Tiger Doyle, limping and mute, Dick Blake with jovial
and eager gaze, Michael Kerrigan and Thomas P. Bolger
flourishing notebooks. Mick's laughing face rose suddenly in
his memory, and the sunlight played on the impassive statue,
on Arthur Macken beside it in a lingering grey-green group;
the sunlight played on the statue and its simple wording:

To Michael Collins, who died for Ireland.

The words of the old heroic tale came back: "And the wind
and the sun flamed before and behind."